Fig. 1.—This rare print, hand-tinted in the original, was published by A. Imbert at 104 Broadway, near Pine St. At a later period Currier, Kellogg and other lithographers copied the print, rendering it as a somewhat crude and garishly-colored caricature. Note the figure at the left representing the "world."

The Gift to be Simple

SONGS, DANCES AND RITUALS
OF THE AMERICAN SHAKERS

By Edward D. Andrews

DOVER PUBLICATIONS, INC.
NEW YORK

TO
FAITH

Published in Canada by General Publishing Company, Ltd., 30 Lesmill Road, Don Mills, Toronto, Ontario.
Published in the United Kingdom by Constable and Company, Ltd., 10 Orange Street, London WC 2.

This Dover edition, first published in 1962, is an unabridged and unaltered republication of the work originally published by J. J. Augustin Publisher in 1940.

International Standard Book Number: 0-486-20022-1

Manufactured in the United States of America
Dover Publications, Inc.
180 Varick Street
New York, N. Y. 10014

CONTENTS

ILLUSTRATIONS

For their constructive criticism of the study in manuscript I am indebted to Dr. George Herzog of Columbia and Dr. George Pullen Jackson of Vanderbilt University. The latter's notes on Shaker musical theory and tune and text relationships were most generously placed at the author's disposal, and his interest in the theme was from the first a stimulus to worthy effort. The early work of Mr. Tom Ryan, of the Little Red School House in New York, several of whose transcriptions are used herein, is greatly appreciated. Especially helpful has been the contribution of Mr. Conrad Held of the South Mountain String Quartet, who not only solved the complexities of certain musical passages but kindly consented to arrange most of the tunes for printing. Lastly, I wish to record the staunch support of Mrs. Lawrence K. Miller, Pittsfield, Mass., who has graciously devoted much time and effort to insuring the success of the present volume.

E. D. A.

Richmond, Mass. May 1, 1940.

This edition is dedicated to the memory of
EDWARD DEMING ANDREWS
1894–1964

THE WORD AUTHORITY, often loosely used to mean one who knows more than most people do about some subject, regains its dignity as soon as we consider Edward Deming Andrews. He knew more about the Shakers than anyone ever has, and I am quite certain that his knowledge of them will never be surpassed. He knew about them; he knew of them; he knew them. His interest in them was many-sided, and indeed was inexhaustible. Not merely their furniture, though that may have been his chief concern, but their songs, their dances, their craftsmanship, their herbs, their drawings, their paintings, their clothes, their manners, their customs, and finally—crown of all—their religion drew out of him a scholarship so dedicated that for purity, for precision, and for completeness it stands alone in our time. He knew the Shakers in this wonderful way because he loved them: not sentimentally, not nostalgically, but with an abiding respect for the ideas their entire life expressed. And he knew how to write of what he so perfectly understood. To enter a room full of Shaker furniture is a unique experience; it takes the breath. But to read one of his books is, to the extent that such a thing now is possible, to inhabit that room.

Mark Van Doren

MARK VAN DOREN

INTRODUCTION

T HE UNITED SOCIETY of Believers in Christ's Second Appearing, commonly called Shakers, had its origin in Bolton and Manchester, England, about the year 1747. Jane Wardley and her husband James, the first leaders of the Lancashire sect, were Quaker tailors who, coming under the influence of the almost extinct French Prophets, perpetuated the continental Camisard teaching that the destruction of the world was imminent and Christ was about to come a second time. Ann Lee, the twenty-two year old daughter of a poor blacksmith in Manchester, was attracted to this group of "shaking Quakers" in 1758, and eventually, by virtue of her gifts of leadership and strange visions and revelations, assumed a dominant rôle in the movement. In 1772, after being imprisoned for disturbing the sabbath and publicly preaching her doctrine of celibacy, she was given the title of "Mother" and accepted by a few disciples as the reincarnation of the Christ spirit.

Pious, introspective, mystical, Ann had spent a tragic youth in the textile mills of the manor, acutely sensitive to the omnipresent spectacle of poverty and degradation. Day and night she brooded over the nature of sin until her health, both mental and physical, was seriously undermined. She became subject to wild outbursts of emotion, to visions, dark forebodings and vague messianic delusions. Shaken by despair at the evil of life and by doubts of her own salvation, John Lee's daughter found solace only in the companionship and heretical doctrines of the Wardleys. Her particular obsession—that sexual intercourse was the root of all sin—seems not to have become fixed, however, until after her marriage to Abraham Stanley, a Manchester blacksmith.

She had taken this step against her will, and the death in infancy of the four children born of the union was to her the act of an angry God. Her earlier prejudices against carnal relationships now developed into a monomania. In vision she witnessed the act by which Adam and Eve fell from their primal purity. She held converse with the Lord Jesus himself, who commissioned her to fulfil the work of redemption which He had begun. On coming from the prison where she had been thus "anointed," she boldly proclaimed she was "Ann the Word," the Bride of the Lamb, that the day of judgment was at

[3]

hand, and that salvation was possible only by confessing and forsaking all fleshly practices. A sacred ecclessia, later to be known as the millennial or resurrection church, gathered together under her banner, holding secret meetings where the members danced with the ecstasy of a chosen and exalted people.

Directed by a revelation from heaven and provided with resources by John Hocknell, the only well-to-do member of the society, nine members of the order came to America in 1774. The prophetess found temporary employment in New York, where her husband deserted her for another woman. Her brother William (Father William) and her chief "apostle" James Whittaker (Father James) accompanied Hocknell to Albany, near which town, in the wilderness of Niskeyuna (later Watervliet, N. Y.) they purchased a small tract of land. In 1776, the first year of the Revolution, Ann rejoined the little community which had been established up the Hudson river.

For four years little progress was made in spreading the "true" gospel. The initial .mpetus was provided by a New Light Baptist revival in New Lebanon, N. Y., near the Massachusetts line, whose subjects, seeking a definite way to salvation, were attracted to the Shaker colony in 1780. There they found a fellowship literally following the example of the primitive apostolic church: men and women living together in celibate purity, holding all goods in common, working industriously with their hands, speaking and singing in unknown tongues, worshipping joyfully, preaching that Christ had actually come to lead believers to a perfect, sinless, everlasting life—the life of the spirit.

From that time on the sect rapidly gained adherents. The imprisonment of Ann and her chief elders on charges of pacifism and treason served to attract further notice to the dissenters. On their release they embarked on a two-year mission through various parts of Massachusetts, Connecticut and New York, constantly proselyting, forming small groups of Believers, and in spite of persecution and abuse, cementing a union dedicated to a life of primitive rectitude. When Mother Ann died in 1784, the foundations had been laid for four colonies in Massachusetts, at Hancock, Tyringham, Harvard and Shirley; two in Maine, at Alfred and New Gloucester (Sabbathday Lake); two in New Hampshire, at Enfield and Canterbury (East Canterbury); one in Enfield, Connecticut; and two in New York, at Watervliet and New Lebanon. The first Shaker meeting-house was erected at New Lebanon in 1785-6 under the direction of James Whittaker (1751-1787), who succeeded Mother Ann as head of the sect.

The organization of the millennial church into communities holding a "joint interest" or common property was the work of an American convert, "Father" Joseph Meacham (1742-1796) of Enfield, Connecticut. Under his able administration the eleven original societies were divided into five bishoprics, each with its own ministry responsible to the "lead" at New Lebanon. Each society patterned its government on the example of the central society, which was subdivided into several family groups controlled by subordinate officers and named (East family, South family, etc.) according to their location from the central Church, the order in which the meeting-house itself was situated. Each family was an independent economic unit consisting of from thirty to perhaps a hundred members, governed by an order of two elders and two eldresses who had the spiritual care of the group and oversight of all the family's affairs. An order of deacons and deaconesses was directly responsible for temporal concerns, while one or more trustees held the consecrated property of the unit. Family leaders were appointed and supervised at New Lebanon by an all powerful, self-perpetuating central ministry composed of two elders and two eldresses, and in the other societies by the branch ministries.

Newcomers were received into the "gathering family" or novitiate order, where they were allowed to retain their own property and family relationships. In the next class or "junior order" they dedicated the use only of their property, which was returnable if the member withdrew; but in the highest order, the church family, the consecration of time, service, talent and property was an irrevocable step solemnly sealed by signing the church covenant. Children were indentured to the deacons or trustees and placed in the "children's order" under a special caretaker. Union of the various groups was achieved by common customs and practices, a common code of manuscript statutes, worship in common on the sabbath day, and a strongly centralized system of government.

The relatively simple elements of Ann's mystic faith were developed by Joseph Meacham into a more consistent and elaborate belief. His was the doctrine of the four "dispensations," those periods in the history of man (from Adam to Abraham to Moses to Jesus to Ann) during which God had gradually unfolded His plan of salvation. The principle of equality of the sexes had been established by the prophetess, who compared her position as head of the true church to that of a wife after the husband (i.e. Jesus) was gone; but Meacham put the principle into actual communal practice, elevating a woman (Lucy Wright) to leadership over the sisterhood and appointing women to positions of equal privilege and responsibility. The doctrine of a dual Deity, or masculine-feminine Godhead, though a logical extension of the concepts of a dual messiah and a coordinate sexual order, seems not to have been expressly formulated until Benjamin Youngs wrote the standard work on Shaker theology, "The Testimony of Christ's Second Appearing," first printed in 1808. In "A Summary View of the Millennial Church" (1823), the doctrines of the manifestation of the Christ spirit in Mother Ann, "spiritual regeneration" and "the new birth" were further clarified. The seven principles of the church of Christ, according to the authors of this work, were duty to God, duty to man, separation from the world, practical peace, simplicity of language, right use of property and the virgin life. These formed the practical and external law of a life based on the twelve christian virtues of faith, hope, honesty, continence, innocence, simplicity, meekness, humility, prudence, patience, thankfulness and charity.

"Mother" Lucy Wright (1760-1821) succeeded Meacham as first in the central ministry. During her administration the movement was extended to Ohio and Kentucky, where eventually six permanent communities were founded: four in Ohio, Union Village (originally Turtle Creek), Watervliet (also called Beulah or Beaver Creek) and Whitewater, all in the southwestern part of the state, and North Union, near Cleveland; and two in Kentucky, South Union in the south of the state and Pleasant Hill, near Harrodsburg. A colony at Busro, near Vincennes, Indiana, was in existence from 1810 to 1827. In 1826 another community was organized at Sodus (Sodus Bay, Port Bay, or Sodus Point) in New York, being transferred ten years later to Groveland or Son Yea in Livingston county.

During the second quarter of the last century the United Society reached its maximum growth with a total membership of about six thousand. After the Civil War, due to a variety of social, economic and religious causes and conflicts, both internal and external, the order began to decline until at the present day there are less than one hundred Shakers in the country. These are distributed in four communities: New Lebanon, Hancock, Canterbury and Sabbathday Lake. The order has refused to compromise on its basic tenets of celibacy and community of goods, preferring to follow a cycle which they say is inevitable for all institutions. Few converts have been made in decades, admissions consisting chiefly of orphans or children placed in the society by parents or guardians. For some time industries have been at low ebb, and the large acreage of the society is cultivated, if at all, by hired labor. Though the temper of an industrial age has left this semi-monastic culture behind, it may yet be claimed that the Shakers represent the oldest, most successful, and most consistently pure communism in the new world, and that their experiment in primitive Christianity has been replete with lessons of value to all mankind.

In the present study the songs, tunes and dances of the sect are discussed in separate sections. It should be noted, however, that in Shaker worship they were inseparable forms of expressing praise, joy, yearning or union. The first Believers were seized by such ecstasy of spirit that, like leaves in the wind, they were moved into the most disordered exercises: running about the room, jumping, shaking, whirling, reeling, and at the same time shouting, laughing or singing snatches of song. No form existed: someone would impulsively cry out a line from the psalms, part of a hymn, or a phrase—perhaps in an unknown tongue— bespeaking wild emotion; someone might prophesy; another would exhort his listeners to repentance; another might suddenly start whirling like a dervish; then, as in a Quaker meeting, all for a time would be silent. After an order of worship was instituted, songs were sung without movement and dances paced without songs, but usually the procedure deliberately duplicated what had originally been involuntary: songs were danced, and the measures of the dance accentuated by the rhythms of the song.

Shaker ritualism was a true folk art. Though the tunes, songs, marches, ring dances and other forms of devotional "exercises" were composed by individuals, they were intended for communal use. Their character and form were peculiarly social: the songs reflected in content the thought and aspiration of the whole group; their tempo was adapted to prescribed parts of the service and dance techniques which the eighteen societies had all adopted in common. The same songs spread through the scattered branches of the order. They were perfected in the week-day singing meetings of the families and bequeathed to the community in the united sabbath worship. They were exchanged among different families. Hundreds were composed as gifts to particular elders or eldresses, or to beloved brothers or sisters. Popular pieces such as "Come life Shaker life," " 'Tis the Gift to be Simple" and "My Carnal Life I will Lay Down" became authentic symbols of a distinct folk culture.

In no other way, in fact, could the restrained Shaker spirit find such freedom of expression. The Believer was disciplined to a precise and simplified functionalism in the crafts; in industry he followed strict routines and tra-

[7]

ditions; he was inhibited by the doctrinal taboos on recreation, reading, and intercourse with the world and the opposite sex; the normal sex impulses were suppressed by the great basic principle of the faith. But in the songs and operations of worship the urge to play, to love, to create, found release in ways which revealed the very soul of the individual and the essential ethos of the sect.

The title of the book is taken from an early song beginning:

> 'Tis the gift to be simple
> 'Tis the gift to be free,
> 'Tis the gift to come down
> Where we ought to be. . . .*

Simplicity was one of the most pervasive of Shaker virtues. In their "travel" towards perfection, the conduct of the Believers, particularly in the processes of worship, was invested with a curious primitivism and child-like innocence. Often their ways were naive and unworldly. But "gospel simplicity" appeared in aspects more mature: as Christian humility, the product of self-discipline and self-denial; as singleness of purpose, giving vitality to work and deed; as a doctrine of purity, affecting the labour of the hands. Speech and dress bore the impress of plainness. Thought and policy were honest and direct. In various guises the quality was ever-present, an essential attribute of the unity, harmony and consecration of a unique religious order.

The term "gift," so common in Shaker usage, likewise had its origin in the scriptures. "There are diversities of gifts," wrote Paul to the Corinthians—miracles, prophecy, discerning of spirits, unknown tongues, "diversities of operations"—but "the same spirit . . . the same God which worketh all in all."

*See song No. 72.

I

SONGS AND RITUALS

The first Shaker "songs" were wordless tunes. In their meetings at Manchester, on board the ship "Mariah" which took them to America, and at the early preaching stations in the new world, the Believers had no hymns, anthems or spiritual songs expressive of their new-born faith. Taboo were the songs they were accustomed to sing: the anthems of the established sects, the "carnal" verses of British marches, hunting songs, popular ballads and other secular compositions. Singing was either a droning of fragments from the psalms, a babble of "unknown tongues," shouts and outcries of "ho, ho," "halleluiah," etc., or such random sing-song as "do, do, diddle, do" and "too-ral-loo."

However, the "gift" of song, a genuine song consciousness, was present even at the beginning of the movement. The great afflatus which swept the first assemblies found vent in a vociferous if uncoordinated activity. At their frequent meetings they sang and danced far into the night. The three "witnesses," Mother Ann Lee, Father William Lee and Father James Whittaker, often led their followers in "solemn songs" of their own making. Visitors to the swampland community at Niskeyuna frequently came upon the prophetess as she was humming, "in a melodious voice," some strange sad tune.

The earliest account of Shaker singing is found in a small pamphlet, "Some Brief Hints, of a Religious Scheme,"[1] first published in Norwich (Conn.) in 1781. Its author, Valentine Rathbun, was a Baptist minister from Pittsfield (Mass.) who had joined the sect in 1780 and apostasized after a few months of disgruntled membership. Describing the mode of worship, Rathbun wrote:

Some will be singing, each one his own tune; some without words, in an Indian tone, some sing jig tunes, some tunes of their own making, in an unknown mutter, which they call new tongues....

In the Salem (1782) edition of this pamphlet the subject is somewhat amplified. The singing began, the author reported, after a violent shaking or jerking of the head from side to side. The eyes were closed. Then

[1] For complete title, see bibliography.

[9]

one will begin to sing some odd tune, without words or rule; after a while another will strike in; and then another; and after a while they all fall in, and make a strange charm:— Some singing without words, and some with an unknown tongue or mutter, and some with a mixture of English: The mother, so called, minds to strike such notes as make a concord, and so form the charm.[2] When they leave off singing, they drop off, one by one, as oddly as they come on.

At a meeting at Harvard in 1782, William Plumer, later governor of New Hampshire, heard individuals in the midst of the dance cry out "ho, ho," or "Love, love," whereupon the whole assembly would vehemently clap their hands; "at other times some were shaking and trembling, others singing words out of the Psalms in whining, canting tones (but not in rhyme)."[3]

"Worded" songs did not appear until the English Shaker church, with its Quaker background, had become impregnated with the spirit of early American revivalism. There were two consecutive and closely related streams of influence:

(1) The first communities of Believers in New York and New England grew, directly or indirectly, out of conditions created by "the great awakening," that tremendous upheaval which resulted in the formation of the liberal, anti-Calvinistic or New Light doctrine. The New Light and Free Will churches, particularly the Baptists, were still holding powerful revivals when the Shakers came upon the scene, though in many places the movement was on the wane and hundreds of its subjects had become disillusioned about the second coming of their Lord. Under such circumstances the gospel of Ann Lee held out to them a renewed promise and an actual program of salvation. Flocking to the Shaker banner from all parts of the Northeast, these communicants of older faiths brought with them the lively songs and folk-hymns which were part of New Light worship.

(2) Two decades later the process was repeated in Kentucky and Ohio. The leaders at New Lebanon saw in the Kentucky Revival, which opened in 1799-1800, a dual opportunity: the redemption of "lost souls" and the expansion of Shaker influence. In 1805 they sent to this distant field three of their ablest missionaries, whose work was so successful that eventually seven societies were

---

[2] Apparently this means that Mother Ann set the pitch.

[3] The Original Shaker Communities in New England. (The Plumer Papers. Frank Sanborn, ed.) In The New England Magazine, New Series, Vol. 22. 1900. Clapping the hands during a dance or song was a common method, even in Plumer's day, of marking the time. In the latter half of the nineteenth century psalms were often set to Shaker music, especially at Canterbury.

established on the western frontier. These communities were composed largely of former "New Lights," "Schismatics" and "Christians" whose rebellion from the orthodoxies of the Baptist, Methodist and Presbyterian faiths had precipitated the Revival. When the members of these churches, like their prototypes in New England, reorganized under the Shaker aegis, they retained not only the exercises and "operations" of revivalism, which were akin to those of the Shakers, but also the primitive songs which had formed an integral part of the backwoods services.

This second contact with New Light song was more productive of results than the first. Perhaps the ascetic and dissenting spirit of the first Shaker congregations had consciously resisted the innovation of sacred song. The nascent communities in Kentucky and Ohio, on the other hand, were organized on a free frontier and at a later period, when the prejudices of the original Believers were becoming somewhat modified. It is possible, furthermore, that the southern Baptists and Methodists had developed the revival song further than their precursors in the north. Under the fluid conditions of an unsettled country, left free to take its natural course, the revival songs would naturally have carried over into the Shaker institution. It should be remembered that at first there were only three representatives in the west of the parent church, the missionaries Benjamin Youngs, Isaachar Bates and John Meacham, whose task was to leaven with Shaker principles all the older faiths attracted to Ann Lee's gospel. Bates himself, as a fifer in the Revolution and a great music-lover, probably welcomed the new songs into the old solemn worship. Youngs was a liberal leader who would not have been averse to revival songs as a means of building up new branches of the church. Most important of all was the fact that one of the leaders of the Revival, Richard McNemar, a former Presbyterian, became the outstanding figure of western Shakerism. A prolific writer, McNemar composed more hymns, anthems and exercise songs for the early order than any other individual.

Once grafted into the Shaker organism, the musical tradition of the Baptists and Methodists immediately throve and bore fruit; for the millennial society was essentially a folk culture, a vigorous independent movement free from many of the restrictions and conventions which bound the established churches. The Believers were faced, however, with the problem of creating an entirely new body of religious song, hymns expressive of their peculiar faith, their status of separateness and "superiority" over all "anti-christian" systems. This problem they solved much as the New Lights and other rebellious sects had done before them, by "plundering the carnal lover" of his tunes, by making over to their own needs existent spiritual and secular songs.[4] As they themselves phrased it in an early hymn:

> Let justice seize old Adam's crew,
> And all the whore's production;
> We'll take the choicest of their songs,
> Which to the Church of God belongs,
> And recompence them for their wrongs,
> In singing their destruction.[5]

On May 23, 1805, at the first regular Shaker service held in the west—at Turtle Creek, later Union Village, in southwestern Ohio—the worshippers united in singing a brief verse:

> With him in praises we'll advance
> And join the virgins in the dance[6]

which is the first true Shaker song to be recorded. By 1806 many hymns composed "in the spirit of the work" were being sent on to the eastern communities, where they were first tried out in the union meetings.[7] Interest in singing became contagious. In the summer of the following year "The Happy Journey"[8] was composed at Watervliet and sung at New Lebanon to the tune of an early

---

[4] See Jackson, George Pullen. Spiritual Folk-Songs of Early America. New York, 1937. In the preface to this informative book, John Powell discusses "the practice of singing religious songs to folk-tunes."

[5] Millennial Praises, Hancock (Mass.), 1813. (Hymn XI, p. 169: "The Saints' Triumph on the Downfall of Antichrist.")

[6] Benjamin Youngs' manuscript "Journal of One Year, Jan. 1, 1805 to Dec. 31, 1805." Author's library.

[7] It was Joseph Meacham's belief that "male and female were so created that they *would* have a union together"—and that if it was not in the spirit then it would be in the flesh. To promote *spiritual* union between the sexes, therefore, he instituted in 1793 the "union meeting"—one of the basic social customs of the sect. Following a prescribed order set by the ministry, an equal number of brethren and sisters met two evenings a week and twice on Sundays in certain retiring-rooms; sat facing each other in two ranks about five feet apart; and conversed for about an hour, each with the person opposite him or her, on topics of mutual but impersonal interest. Sometimes the gathering was turned into a singing meeting.

[8] For tune and words, see song No. 6. In "Millennial Praises," the first printed hymnal of the sect, the song (Hymn XXI, Part II) was expanded to eleven verses.

solemn song. "Gospel Trumpet,"[9] written about the same time and set to a distinct lively movement, was likewise expressive of a renewed animation of the Shaker spirit, the direct result of the western revival and a new influx of "young Believers in the east." Soon the solemn wordless songs were being dropped and words provided for the early tunes and "exercise songs." About 1810 "little songs" or short anthems, called "extra songs,"[10] found a place in the worship of both the eastern and western divisions of the church. Longer anthems came into use about 1812.

Up to the time of the Kentucky revival, the limited number of Shaker tunes could be learned by rote or "hearing." But to remember the longer "noted" and "worded" songs and sing them correctly, some knowledge of music was required. In Youngs' words, the reading of music, "gradually introduced about 1807," was made necessary because of the labor involved in "retaining" and "conveying" an increasing repertoire of hymns.[11] It was not until 1815, however, that the first anthem "with music attached," a piece called "Mother's children,"[12] was brought out at New Lebanon. Four years later a "packet" of "scored" songs, so-called, was sent from Ohio to New Lebanon and another returned, an exchange of spiritual greetings which would have been less complete without the written note.

From this time on, the importance of an understanding of musical notation, against which the first Shakers were prejudiced, was officially recognized. One Abram Whitney, a former music teacher and member of the Shirley society, began to teach theory and practice at Shirley, Harvard, Canterbury and other communities. About 1820, hymns introduced by melodic lines began to appear in Shaker manuscript hymnals; and in 1823, two years after he was appointed superintendent of schools in the first bishopric (New Lebanon, Hancock and Watervliet), Seth Y. Wells began to encourage instruction in singing and music, recommending that a half hour each day be devoted to that purpose. Early in the 1820's popular interest in music was stimulated by the Harvard society's experiments in a new system of notation.[13]

[9] Hymn XV, Part II in Millennial Praises.

[10] "Being sung promiscuously, or in addition to the appointed songs and the usual exercise songs." (Youngs, Isaac N. A Concise View of the Church of God and of Christ, on Earth, Having its foundation in the faith of Christ's First and Second Appearing, New Lebanon, 1856. MS. Hereafter this document will be referred to as the Youngs manuscript.)

[11] Youngs MS.

[12] The text may be found in Millennial Praises, pp. 188-189.

[13] See p. 87 ff.

An examination of the 140 compositions in the first Shaker hymnal—"Millennial Praises," published in 1812 and 1813—discloses the source of a few of the Believers' songs. There are at least ten hymns, as Professor Jackson has pointed out, "which (a) are found widely in the contemporary books of the other separatist sects mentioned above or (b) are more or less clear textual adaptations of such borrowed songs."[14] Three hymns, "Voyage to Canaan,"[15] "Babylon is fallen"[16] and "The Journey to Canaan,"[17] were appropriated by the Shakers and used practically unchanged. Adaptations or parodies include "The foundation Pillars revealed,"[18] "The only Way,"[19] "The happy Day,"[20] "Old Adam disturbed,"[21] "The Day long prayed for,"[22] "Come and welcome"[23] and "The Hiding place."[24]

These songs and probably several more, as yet unidentified, seem to have seeped into Shaker lyrism, as we have noted, from the Baptist "merry dancers" and other "new light" orders in the east, as well as from those sects which participated in the Great Southern and Western Revival. A perusal of Shaker hymns written or published in the twenty-year period after the appearance of "Millennial Praises" reveals a few, though an ever-decreasing number of deriva-

[14] Correspondence of Prof. George Pullen Jackson, Vanderbilt University.

[15] Hymn X, Part I, beginning "A people called Christians." Cf. Jackson, Spiritual Folk Songs of America, No. 136, "Spiritual Sailor." "Voyage to Canaan," like "Spiritual Sailor," was probably sung to the ancient "Stormy Winds do Blow" tune.

[16] Hymn XXIII, Part I, beginning, "Hail the day so long expected!" Cf. Jackson, ibid., No. 192.

[17] Hymn XVII, Part IV, beginning, "The old Israelites knew." Cf. Jackson, "Down East Spirituals" (unpublished), No. 31.

[18] Hymn IV, Part I, beginning "Blow ye the trump in Zion." Cf. Jackson, "Spiritual Folk Songs of Early America," the songs entitled "Wedlock" Nos. 13 and 43).

[19] Hymn XII, Part I, beginning "Salvation is a joyful sound." Cf. Jackson, "Down East Spirituals," No. 165. Also Watts.

[20] Hymn XIV, Part I, beginning "How happy the day, when the new living way." Cf. Jackson, ibid., No. 125, beginning "O how happy are they who their Saviour obey."

[21] Hymn XXIV, Part I, beginning "Man in his first creation." Cf. Jackson, "Spiritual Folk Songs of Early America," Nos. 13 and 43, and "Down East Spirituals," No. 56. Both Shaker and non-Shaker songs are "Adam songs" on the marriage theme, "the former decrying it, the latter defending it, both backing up their arguments by scriptural witness." (Jackson.) Dr. Jackson believes the "Wedlock" form of tune could have been used for a number of "creation" songs in "Millennial Praises."

[22] Hymn II, Part IV, beginning "The prophets they look'd for the day." Cf. Jackson, "Down East Spirituals," No. 47, for stanzaic pattern resemblances.

[23] Hymn VIII, Part IV, beginning "Come, ye sinners, come and welcome." Cf. Jackson, "Spiritual Folk Songs of Early America," No. 239, beginning "Come ye sinners, poor and needy."

[24] Hymn III, Part IV, beginning "Hail precious truth! thou living way." Cf. Jackson, "Down East Spirituals," No. 35. In the Shaker version as in the down-east song, most stanzas end with the words "hiding place."

tions. In George DeWitt's manuscript hymnal,[25] dated 1822, we find "The Humble Heart"[26] (the melody of which is surely a derivation), as well as an example of the once-current shaped notes.[27] Another "Collection of Hymns and Spiritual Songs" (MS.), compiled at New Lebanon in 1830, contains a parody of Burns' "And A' That" and was probably sung to the original Scotch tune. In the second book of hymns to be published, McNemar's "A Selection of Hymns and Poems; For the use of Believers" (Watervliet, Ohio, 1833) we again encounter "Babylon is Fallen" (Babylon's Fall) as well as "The Gospel-Trumpet,"[28] songs widely used in American revival circles of the period. Later, in "A Collection of Millennial Hymns," published at Canterbury in 1847, there are two songs, "Deceitfulness of Earthly Joy," beginning "How short are the pleasures of earthly enjoyment!," and "The Holy Savior," beginning "There came forth a voice, to the lost child of nature," both of which were evidently parodies of "The Old Oaken Bucket" and sung to that tune. The Canterbury song, "Lamb's Title" ("Come little children now you may"), in the same collection, is found in non-Shaker circles.[29] In the chapter on tunes we shall have occasion to mention a few other songs or melodies, obviously non-Shaker in origin, which were heard by visitors attending meetings during the first half of the last century.

On the other hand, the very fewness of these borrowings—few in relation to the extensive number of Shaker hymns—indicates that the Believers, even at first, insulated themselves rather completely from the melodic and textual material which was all about them. As time went on, Shaker hymn texts lacked more and more those conventions "in metric verse and stanzaic form . . . which allowed their being sung to the traditional tunes of the non-Shaker folk, the result being the gradual disappearance of such tunes from their collection."[30] The scarcity of outright borrowings and the snatches of tunes and texts in these collections suggest that the Shaker hymn writers did little more than take an

[25] Written at New Lebanon, this hymnal (containing 30 tunes and 115 texts) is the second oldest document in the author's collection, and the first to include tunes. The oldest book of hymn texts was commenced by one David Slosson at the same community in 1808, only twenty-four years after the death of Ann Lee.

[26] See song No. 8.

[27] See Fig. 9.

[28] Cf. the common revival song, "The Martial Trumpet." Also Jackson, "Down East Spirituals," No. 40.

[29] Cf. Jackson, "Down East Spirituals," No. 140.

[30] Correspondence of Dr. George Pullen Jackson.

occasional hint from other songs, perhaps an opening line or fragment of melody, and then went on into purely Shaker compositions.

The doctrinal and peculiarly Shaker character of the hymns in "Millennial Praises" is indicated by their titles: "The Son and Daughter," "The Heavenly Bridegroom & Bride," "The Virgin Spouse," "The latter Day," "Old Adam disturbed," "Resolution against a carnal Nature," "The Believer's Faith," "Humility," "Mother," "The Believers' Answer," "The Language of the Spirit," "The Living Building," "There are Eunuchs," "The Tree of Life," etc. "Typical Dancing," the first two verses of which are given below, has a characteristic meter:

> The Israelites, when they got free,
> From Pharaoh's land, in haste did flee,
> And on the banks of the Red Sea,
> A joyful scene commenced;
> An Elder sister led the band,
> With sounding timbrel in her hand,
> While virgins move by her command,
> And after her they danced.
>
> At Shiloh was a yearly feast,
> Where virgins met from west to east;
> These virgins were a type, at least
> Of those that follow Jesus;
> If they went forth in dances then,
> Why should our dancing now offend,
> Since from the filthy lusts of men,
> Our blessed Saviour frees us?

Though replete with Shaker ideas, these first hymns and anthems were stirring songs. The Believers were out to condemn the flesh, root and branch, and their rhymed diatribes against the evils of a carnal nature were born of fierce conviction. Shaking was "no foolish play," "Judgment's work" was going on, the "flames of truth" were blazing. It was "a day of separation," an issue of damnation or eternal life.

Yet the songs were often cheerful, as in "Joyful Worship:"

> We love to sing and dance we will
> Because we surely, surely feel
> It does our thankful spirits fill
> With heavenly joy and pleasure....

or "the Season of Loves:"

> What beautiful songs do I hear!
> How sweet is the season of loves!
> When Father and Mother are near,
> We feel like a parcel of doves. . . .

There were songs also like "Mother,"[31] which recounted in narrative form the trials, adventures and triumphs of Ann Lee and the millennial church. McNemar's "Selection of Hymns and Poems"[32] provides an index of those compositions current, especially in the western societies, in the twenty-year period after "Millennial Praises" was issued. "The Soul and Sensual Principle Separated" is typical of the prevailing thought. Memorial hymns or elegies, funeral anthems, welcome songs and Christmas and New Year hymns were common. A favorite form was the dialogue or colloquy: "Little-faith & Go-ahead," "Clear-sight & Double-eyes," "The Church & the Old Gentlemen," etc. Such songs as "Industry and Economy," "Industry," "The Steamboat," "Slug"[33] and "Hoggish Nature" were curiously didactic. A purely educative purpose was served by a "Covenant Hymn" (into which the basic principles of the Shaker covenant were incorporated) and by "A Declaration of Junior Membership." "A Good Resolution" is a characteristic march:

> I mean to be obedient,
> And cross my ugly nature,
> And share the blessings that are sent
> To ev'ry honest creature;
> With ev'ry gift I will unite
> And join in sweet devotion:—
> To worship God is my delight,
> With hands and feet in motion.

[31] This popular ballad-like song, beginning "Let names and sects and parties Accost my ears no more," is given in full on pp. 47-51. Composed by Richard McNemar, it was later reprinted in pamphlet form.

[32] The compiler's name is given as "Philos Harmoniae," which was the pseudonym of Richard McNemar. Though published nearly fifteen years after notes began to appear in the manuscript hymnals, the booklet has no music: a fact not to be wondered at, as music type was difficult to set and the order had by then adopted a letter notation not easily rendered in printed form.

[33] There was no place in a Shaker community for "old slug," the traditional name for a lazy or sluggish fellow.

Also:

> Now's the time to travel on
> Now's the time to labor
> Now's the time for every one
> To be a good Believer.
> Don't be dry—don't be dry—
> Now's the time to gather—
> Come and drink! Come and drink
> Drink and live forever.

The above songs may have been danced to the tune of "Yankee Doodle"—an early favorite of the church—and repeated over and over again. Repetitions were common in the Shaker dance song, with no pauses between the stanzas.

Few of the pieces in either of these hymn-books retained for long their original popularity. The Shakers never confined themselves to a particular kind of spiritual song, believing that all aspects of worship should be "limited to the period of their usefulness." As Seth Wells explained in his foreword to Millennial Praises, "words are but the signs of our ideas and of course must vary as the ideas increase with the increasing work of God."

Not published in "Millennial Praises" or "A Selection of Hymns and Poems," but popular within the same period, were a number of so-called "eccentric" songs, usually sung in meetings not open to the world. In content and spirit, as well as in the manner in which they were rendered, these expressive pieces were nearer the folk-level, more akin to the songs which the Revival of 1837 was to produce than the orthodox verses in the Hancock and Watervliet collections. Often, as in the following "Great I" song, the singing was accompanied by gestures or pantomime, in this case expresssive of hatred of pride, flesh and the devil:

1. The *devil* in walking the earth to and fro,
   Has *stamped* the whole human race;
   This awful *impression* believers do know,
   Great I in the *front* of the face.

2. Since Mother has taught me that this is the case,
   No more I'll be deceived with a lie,
   But now from my forehead I'll quickly erase
   The *stamp* of the devil's great I.

3. Come brethren and sisters, pull low and pull high
   Pull away with a free heart and hand;
   O pull away, pull away, pull down great I,
   Then we who are little may stand—[34]

In the last line of the first verse the singers would point to or place their hands on their foreheads; in the third line of the next stanza they would furiously pluck the devil's "stamp" from the same spot; and during the last verse all would make the motions of hauling a rope as on shipboard.

The Shakers stamped and grimaced as they shouted the fifth line of an early "gospel relation" song:

> I love my faithful brethren more
> Than any souls I've seen before;
> Their spirits are so clean and pure,
> They are so kind and clever:
> I love to see them *stamp* and *grin,*
> And curse the flesh, the seat of sin,
> To all such souls I feel akin,
> I will love them forever.

In a popular "warring song" of the period, the repeated phrases "she wars" and "I'll war" were emphasized by motions similar to those of a man mowing:

> My Mother is a valiant warrior,
> *She wars, she wars, she wars,*
> And overcomes and conquers all evil.
>
> I will be like Mother,
> *I'll war, I'll war, I'll war* the flesh,
> And overcome and conquer and reign with my Mother.

Heads were bowed when the words "supple my neck" and "easy yoke" were sung in the following:

> My old fleshly nature I'll torture and vex
> I'll humble my pride and *supple my neck;*
> Never flinch at the cross, have my stubborn will broke,
> Till I am accustomed to Christ's easy yoke,
> *Easy yoke, easy yoke,*
> Till I am accustomed to Christ's easy yoke.

[34] Haskett, William J. Shakerism Unmasked, or the History of the Shakers, pp. 185-186. Pittsfield, 1828. Words underlined were emphasized or shouted. Cf. "Dismission of Great I," p. 79.

The antithesis of "I love my faithful brethren more" was a famous song which, it was alleged, was taught to the Shaker children at an early day. It was not allowed to be sung before "the world's people":[35]

Gospel Relation.

1. My gospel relations are dearer to me
   Than all the flesh kindred that ever I see:
   So good and so pretty, so cleaver they feel;
   To see them & love them increases my zeal,
      O how pretty they look!
      How pretty they look!
      How cleaver they feel!

2. My brethren & sisters, wherever they be
   I always can feel them a treasure to me;
   So good and so pretty, so cleaver they feel,
   To see them & love them increases my zeal.
      O how pretty they look!
      How pretty they look!
      How cleaver they feel!

3. Of all the good friends that I ever possess
   I certainly love good believers the best
   So good & so pretty so cleaver they feel
   To see them and love them increases my zeal.
      O how pretty they look!
      How pretty they look!
      How cleaver they feel!

4. Of all the relation that ever I see
   My old fleshly kindred are furthest from me,
   So bad and so ugly, so hateful they feel
   To see them and hate them increases my zeal.
      O how ugly they look!
      How ugly they look!
      How nasty they feel!

[35] In explaining this song, which was inconsistent with a doctrine of brotherly love, the later Shaker leaders would say, in fact did say, that it was the carnal spirit *in* the worldly relations of the Believers which they were taught to shun and despise.

FIG. 2.—The first Shaker meeting-houses in New York and New England were gambrel-roofed.
In the background, above, is the first church of the Believers, built at New Lebanon in 1785.
The larger "barrel-roofed" structure which replaced this building was raised in 1822. The two
doors facing the street were for the use of the "world's people." The Shakers themselves entered
at the "porch" or wing, the brethren at the right door and the sisters at the left. The central door
was reserved for the ministry, whose rooms were in the upper lofts.

The traditional Sabbath morning or afternoon service, as well as the evening worship of the separate families, was preceded by a period called "retiring-time," during which all members retired to their rooms for a half-hour of meditation, or to refresh their minds on the hymns to be sung at the ensuing meeting. If the assembly was to be in the meeting-house, the families would march to the "Church order" in files of two, the elders in the lead, the sisters following the brethren. The latter would enter the church by one door (the right), the sisters the other, and silently take their places, according to position and age, on long benches so arranged that the sexes would face each other in parallel ranks. After sitting awhile in silence, in the manner of the Quakers, the worshippers would arise at a signal from the preacher or presiding elder, who sat where the rows of benches almost converged. The benches being removed, the meeting would customarily open with a devotional hymn, followed by a discourse directed as much, perhaps, to the public as to the followers of the faith.

Marches and dance songs were sung and "labored" after the meeting had got well under way. Whereas the hymns and anthems voiced the doctrines of the sect, the exercise songs expressed its inner spirit. Usually, at the beginning of the meeting, the rounds and marches were ceremoniously performed; but as we shall see, orderly services sometimes turned into what was called "a quick meeting," or "Shaker high," when dancing would return to its earlier, the "back" or "promiscuous" form, and the singing, regardless of spectators, partake of a substance and quality not provided for in the printed hymnals.

Song-writing was greatly stimulated by the great revival which, breaking out without warning in the fall of 1837, held all the communities in its mysterious thrall for more than a decade. Though the "spirituals" of this extraordinary period carried on the traditions established by the earlier songs, certain differences should be noted. The first Shaker hymns were deliberately composed by the few; many tunes were borrowed; and most of the songs used in communal worship were either printed or had been memorized. The songs of the Great Revival, on the other hand, were produced by the many, appearing in such numbers that, for purposes of use and preservation, the ministry directed that all be recorded in written hymnals.[36] Many were spontaneously composed, often under circumstances which made it necessary for a second person, either a

[36] Many of these manuscript books, simply bound in calf, are beautifully written. Sometimes the paper is a pale blue.

"scribe" or the recipient of the "gift," to record the words and tune. Coming into being thus, both text and melody had a specific indigenous quality, often lacking those conventions in metric verse and stanzaic form which allowed their being sung to non-Shaker tunes. Some of the tunes, in fact, were little more than note-sequences, hardly melodies at all in the strict sense of the word.[37] Considered as a body, the "manifestation songs" are pure Shaker, a distinct offshoot from the main stock of American religious folk-song. So unorthodox were they, indeed, that after the revival was over none were printed in the several hymnals published by the society.[38]

Authorship of the songs of the manifestations was usually ascribed to transcendental sources. Some were cherished as sacred messages or gifts from the ethereal lips of Mother Ann herself. Others came from early leaders of the church, departed members, biblical saints, or figures famous in history who had entered the Shaker heaven. Still others were received from the Heavenly Father, Holy Mother Wisdom,[29] the Saviour, or angels with resounding names. Many were consigned by the sender to particular individuals or groups, either the recipient of the song or a third party. Composed under the mystical influence of such spirits, they reflected in various ways the exalted temper of the time.

[37] In a letter to the author, Dr. Jackson voices the opinion that this "plethora of note sequences" was due in part to the scattering of Believers in separate family units. The songs therefore had "little chance for that wide singing which tends to conventionalize those that are liked and to eliminate those which do not meet with general approval." Though nearly every song-utterance was recorded, many of them were probably seldom sung, even in the families where they were "received."

[38] Since the middle of the nineteenth century the Shakers have published eleven hymnals, all of which, with the exception of "A Sacred Repository of Anthems and Hymns" (Canterbury, 1852) were provided with the round notes of standard usage. (See bibliography.)

[39] In the Shaker concept of a dual deity, Holy Mother Wisdom was co-equal with the Heavenly Father. God created man in his own image: "male and female created he them." "Hence it must appear evident," wrote Seth Wells in his "Summary View of the Millennial Church," "that there exists in the DEITY, the likeness of male and female, forming the unity of that creative and good principle from which proceeds the work of *Father* and *Mother*, manifested in *Power* to create, and *Wisdom* to bring forth into proper order, all the works of God." (A Summary View of the Millennial Church, p. 92.) In the preface to Paulina Bates' "The Divine Book of Holy and Eternal Wisdom" (Canterbury, 1849, p. IV) Wisdom is called "the Mother, or Bearing Spirit of all the works of God," because such works were revealed "through the line of the female (i.e. Ann Lee), being Wisdom's Likeness."

The Shakers placed their "sacred parentage" into three groups: "Our Heavenly Parents," signifying Christ and Mother Ann; "Our Spiritual Parents," implying "the parents in Church relation," Father Joseph Meacham, Mother Lucy Wright and others; and "Our Eternal Parents," applying to Almighty God and Holy Mother Wisdom.

The songs produced at New Lebanon, Watervliet, Hancock and other places at the beginning of this era were called "vision" or "gift" songs. Coming as gifts from the spiritual world, often in visions or trances, they were comparable, in some instances, to the spontaneous "songs" or outcries of the revival meetings in Ohio and Kentucky thirty years before. The earliest one to be recorded was sung on August 16, 1837, by fourteen-year-old Ann Maria Goff of the South family, or "Gathering Order," at Watervliet. During the day, as she and her girl companions became entranced, some of them began to shake and whirl, and all acted strangely. In the evening, as they lay on their beds, three of the children were "taken under operations," their senses appearing to be "withdrawn from the scenes of time." In this condition Ann Maria began to sing:

> Where the pretty angels dwell, Heaven!
> Where the pretty angels dwell forever.

Whether the child's "song" was later put to music, the records do not say. But many succeeding ones were, the tunes being composed independently or patterned on the mode in which they were originally sung. The character of these early vision songs may be seen from three additional examples, "heard" in October, 1837 by three older sisters of the same Watervliet family:

> O my soul, O my soul
> Wake up, wake up and be thankful
> For thy precious priv'lege in the gospel.
>
> *Eliette Gibbs.*

> Mother says go on dear children,
> Mother says rejoice, rejoice![40]
>
> *Matilda Southwick.*

> How happy pretty little Angels are,
> O How happy.
>
> *Clarissa Shoefelt.*

Mystery cloaks the reception of such songs and tunes. The trance singing of Ann Maria Goff, which ushered in the revival of 1837, soon spread to other

[40] For the tune, see song No. 34.

children, who, after their visits to the spirit land, told their elders of the beautiful songs they had heard. Often the gift would come unexpectedly, when the children were occupied in work or play; or in the night-time, awakening the sleeper like a vivid but exquisite dream. The first evidence of the manifestations at North Union, Ohio, was also through "some young persons" who, on an August day in 1838, while walking on the bank of a creek near the Mill family, "heard some beautiful singing which seemed to be in the air above their heads."

It was not long before old members were similarly affected. Before the year was out "vision songs" were reported, usually by the sisterhood, at Watervliet, New Lebanon, Hancock, Harvard, and eventually all the communities. Early in 1838 the first "negro" songs were being sung by an inspired elder of the Enfield, N. H., colony; and at the Groveland (N. Y.) society, songs in "Indian," "Hotentot," "Chinese" and unknown tongues.[41] The gift[42] might "descend" on a brother, or group of brethren, while they were on a journey, or out on the country roads in their peddler's wagons loaded with Shaker merchandise; or on a group of sisters at work in the wash-house or in the fields gathering herbs. One was "given to the brethren that were splitting wood"; another was learned "while on the mountain blackberrying;" "Kitchen Visit" was sent by the spirit of Mother Lucy "to those that worked in the kitchen;" "Mother's Love" was sung to the sisters "while they were cutting apples."

Occasionally the song was consigned to a certain group such as the order of elders, "the children under 20," or "the children under 25." "Wisdom's Pleasure" was printed "upon a sheet of gold" by Holy Wisdom and brought by Mother Ann for "a special notice to all between 60 and 30." Most of the pieces, however, were intended for special recipients, whose names with other relevant particulars were recorded, in the old manuscript hymnals, at the end of the verses.

Authorship of the vision songs was frequently attributed to Mother Ann or Mother Lucy Wright, perhaps because the "gift" descended chiefly on the sisterhood. Sometimes the Saviour is represented: "Gem of the Morning," for example, sung by Mother Ann and a company of holy angels while marching in the garden of paradise, was copied by the Holy Saviour and given to

[41] See pp. 69-76, also songs 35-38, 42-50.
[42] The word "gift," common in Shaker usage, denoted: (1) some exceptional power or ability, usually of supernatural or divine origin; (2) the exercise or "operation" of such a gift; (3) a spiritual present bestowed by some one in the heavenly spheres; or (4) a direct revelation from God. (See p. 8.) Shaker writers often refer to the biblical "gifts" of healing, miracles, prophecies, "discerning of spirits," "divers kinds of tongues," etc.

Hannah Blake. Holy Mother Wisdom wrote "Wisdom's Harp" on a harp and gave it to the elders of the second order at New Lebanon. Angels with strange names composed or brought many songs: "Eternal Sylvane" was "sung to Mother and the elders while in prison at Albany by a band of angels;" "Al va lan's Trumpet of Praise" was sung "by the holy angel Al va lan together with many of the heavenly hosts to Father Joseph soon after the Church was gathered into holy Order;" "Comforting Trumpet" was brought by an angel "for the pretty little singers for their courage and zeal in learning songs;" and "Pleasant Road" was "given in union with Mother Ann by an Angel of light (Sina Cherub) for Father Joseph's class, by his request." Father Joseph, Father William and Father James were likewise the donors of many songs. A typical number was "Solemn Praise," first sung "in the spiritual world," then "written upon the front side of the box of songs brought by Father James." Usually the visionists heard *directly* from these or other parents in the gospel, though sometimes the song was first confided to another spirit who in turn transmitted it to the earthly vessel. At New Lebanon many gifts were thus received, in 1839, through the agency of Elder Sister Olive Spencer, whose death had occurred five years before her songs were heard. In rare instances, the one who composed the song imagined it had passed through many media in the heavens.

Besides being gifts in themselves, the songs often carried as their message the promise of a celestial reward to the faithful or a recognition of service and fidelity. "O what a pretty treasure Mother has for every one," sung on June 4, 1839 by Electa Blanchard of New Lebanon (who had died in February, 1837), was one of many musical allusions to a compensation for good works. "Beloved Child" was sent by Mother Ann "with the little angel alle van together with her special love and blessing to Sister Desire Sanford for her true faithfulness here below." To this message, the instrument who received (composed) the song adds the note: "Mother says, young brethren and Sisters, I wish to have you notice the zeal and perseverance of my faithful child, behold says Mother what a feeble frame and still what a resolute spirit, bear this on your minds and take example thereby." "The Angels' Blessing" was similarly dedicated to Elder Brother Amos Stower and "I le voo Nee," a song partly in unknown tongue, to Prudence Morrel—"for her faithfulness and the cross she has daily borne." The prevalence of the idea of compensation is suggested by many of the song titles such as "Reward of Pure Love," "Reward of Good Works," "Sure Reward," "Rich Reward," "Reward of Mother," "Reward of Pure Zeal," "Bright

Crown," "Shining Crown," "Crown Never Fading" and "Mother's Present."

The reward is not always in the future. Many songs were accompanied by a spiritual or metaphorical present in the form of a crown, trumpet or beautiful flower symbolical of the love which prompted their bestowal.[43] "Trumpet of Joy," given to Lydia Matthewson of New Lebanon on November 22, 1839, was embellished by Mother Ann with "a gold crown, and placed thereon 5550 stars as a reward for your faithful labors, and the burden you have borne for many years past in the building of Zion." As a reward for her "freedom and simplicity in meeting," Phebe Smith received a spiritual gold chain, an anthem entitled "Gold Chain," and a message which read: "There is 300 links in this chain and they are composed of Faith & good works—in one of these links is placed an anthem which Phebe may have as a reward of well doing." Leah Taylor learned "Mother's Cake of Love" from a cake of love presented to her by the spirit of Mother Ann. Many songs bring or promise "leaves of Mother's love," "sweet roses," "shining gems," "shining bright lamps," "golden seals," boxes of pearls, bugles, doves, white robes, "beautiful robes of comfort and love," and so on. In others—such as "A Mince Pie or a Pudding," "Plum Cake" and "Limber Ointment"—the reward of virtue is a more practical present. Often a song is accompanied by manna, "the wine of Mothers love," an exotic fruit, a precious stone, or perhaps a spiritual harp or other musical instrument. In such visionary experiences the Shakers reached out, like eager children, for the approval, the sensory enjoyment, and the beauty denied them in the rigorous and often arid course of their normal existence.

Another type of gift song was that received from famous (non-Shaker) individuals who had been converted to the faith in the spirit life. In the late 1830's songs received at Canterbury were ascribed to the spirits of George Washington, Thomas Jefferson, William Penn and Christopher Columbus. Washington was supposed to have influenced thousands of spirits to join the eternal Shaker church and to have first conducted the Indians to meetings of the sect.[44] Being a Quaker and also a friend of the Indians on earth, Penn was likewise a favorite figure among the Believers; they admired Jefferson greatly, and for some reason included Columbus in their calendar of saints. The selection of other celebrated characters who visited them was "indiscrimate" and more difficult to explain: President Harrison, Napoleon, Stephen Girard, Mahomet, Leo

[43] See pp. 65-69.
[44] See p. 79.

X, Clement VII, Bishop James Doyle of Ireland, Saint Patrick, Sampson, Alexander the Great, Mary Queen of Scots, Queen Anne, Queen Elizabeth, King Charles II, King George I, King Edwy and Queen Elgiva, General Brock, Marshall Ney, General Bertrand, Nero, Alexander Pope, Osceola, Queen Charlotte, Saint John, King David—these among others. In March, 1839, a "vessel" reported "the first song that Artexerxes received after he embrac'd the gospel; which he received from Mother Ann in the spiritual world." "LaFayette's intercession" was heard after a Sabbath meeting in May, 1839: "Issachar B. (Bates) Sen. came into the room where Zillah Potter was leading a very little spirit by the right hand and it sung the above song. One that (Z. P.) heard LaFayette sing to Mother on his knees."[45]

Equally fantastic circumstances attended a Persian Song in an unknown (non-Persian) tongue, "sent to Elder Sister and Betsey by David Osborn (a deceased brother) on the stem of a garland he brought from Persia." Another piece was "learned from a Nightengale that Susannah Ellis gave to Jonathan Wood." "Watch of the Night" was sung by Mother Ann "at the mid hour of the night thro every room of the dwelling of her Children." "An Indian Song" was given to Brother John M. (Meacham) by an Indian whom he had met "when traveling in the Ohio country." The spirit of Mother Ann communicated "Holy Order" to Father Joseph Meacham "when he had a gift to labor in square order." "Praise to the Most High" was termed "a psalm of David learned of a little spirit of a Nun, by the name of Hellen Augusta Brown that died in Russia." "The Willow" was sung "by Betsy's (Betsy Bates') little Angels they stood on each shoulder with their wings raised." "Jehovah's Call" was "given by a Holy Angel of God by Name, Con-sa-reen." "The Song of Co-lo-vin"—"a little bird of Paradise"—was sung when it came to see its mate, "which had been sent to Elder Sister and Betsy Bates with song some days before." Certain sisters at the Groveland (N. Y.) society learned "From the Moon" while on a visit to that celestial body. The anthem, "My Clear and Holy Jasper," was written upon a stone called "Jasper, the first foundation stone in heavenly Jerusalem." The spirit of John Rodgers, one of Ann's first followers in America, gave to a certain visionist another anthem, "Wisdom's Valley," which had been sung by "a company of 2000 spirits in the swamp of Watervliet, where the church now stands, just one year before the Revolution was commenced in America." "Mes-

[45] LaFayette visited the Watervliet community in 1784. According to Shaker legend, he was converted to the true faith in the spirit world.

senger of Peace" was "printed and pricked in gold letters, then folded and laid in the bottom of a large blue bowl of manna." "Pleasure Song" was "sung and danced on the ridge of the new School house, just after it was raised (Sept. 26, 1839, at New Lebanon) by William Safford," who "attended to the raising with a number more, departed spirits."

In those messages which often accompanied the gift of song, emphasis might be placed on the tune rather than the words. Thus, when Mother Ann sent "Anchor of Safety" to the ministry, she called attention to "a singing harp" which she had placed on the head of Eldress Ruth, "whereon was the tune to the hymn." The tune to "Zion's Watchmen," also given to the ministry, was by a certain Prince Lavinda. When a spiritual instrument of music (commonly a harp or bugle) was received, the one thus favored would often strike up a tune, with words which imitated the sound of the instrument. "The Bugle," received from Daniel's Bugle on a sabbath day in 1839, is a typical example: it had one phrase, "O ho ho ho," repeated over and over again, with a melody something like a bugle call. The sound that "George's Bugle" made was "Vi la hoo hoo hoo!"[46] Sometimes a tune was learned from a scroll carried by a dove, or from a leaf from the tree of songs or the tree of life.[47]

On occasion, spiritual birds attending the heavenly visitant even measured the time of the tune. An eye-witness thus relates:

We were frequently told that some good spirit has entered the room, with a large flock of beautiful birds and doves to time the tune on the head and shoulders of the faithful, when every one . . . that "own the gift," join the bird chorus,—with, peep, peep,—sweet, sweet,—peep, sweet,—boblink, boblink, etc., etc. Those birds often bring instruments of music, and place them on the heads of all in the room. They have a little song they sing in acknowledgment of these presents, one verse reads thus—

> A golden trumpet cross' our heads,
> An instrument of music,
> Attended by a little bird,
> To show us how to use it.[48]

[46] The following note, written beneath "George's Bugle" in the hymnal, explains that this song "was played on Daniel Boler's and Betsy Bates' bugle by George DeWitt & Azuba Tiffany while on the mountain with them and others while absent a blackberrying. Learned the next day by ———— from Azuba Tiffany. Sept., 1839."

[47] See Andrews, Edward D. Shaker Songs. In The Musical Quarterly, October, 1937. New York. See also Fig. 6.

[48] Extract from an unpublished manuscript on Shaker history, (by an eye-witness), giving an

During the period of the so-called "manifestations" many "native" songs were received from Indian spirits or from the shades of Eskimos, Negroes, Abyssinians, Hottentots, Chinese and other races in search of salvation.[49] Squaw songs, and occasionally a papoose song, were common. When Indian spirits came into the Shaker Church, the instruments would become so "possessed" that they sang Indian songs, whooped, danced and behaved generally in the manner of savages. An eye-witness thus describes a meeting which took place at Watervliet in 1843:

> Mother Ann (an instrument reported) has sent two angels to inform us that a tribe of Indians had been around there two days, and wanted the Brothers, and Sisters to take them in . . . the Indians were a savage tribe who had all died before Columbus discovered America; but had been wandering about ever since. . . .
>
> The next dancing night . . . the Elder invited the Indians to come in. . . . The Elders then urged upon the members the duty of 'taking them in' whereupon eight or nine of the Sisters became possessed of the Spirits of Indian Squaws and about six of the Brothers became Indians: then ensued a regular 'Pow Wow,' with whooping, yelling, and strange antics, such as would require a Dickens to describe.
>
> The Sisters and Brothers squatted down on the floor together, Indian fashion, and the Elders, and Eldresses endeavored to keep them asunder. At the same time, telling the Indians that they must be separated from the Squaws, and otherwise instructing them in the rules of Shakerism. Some of the Indians then wanted some 'Suckatash' which was soon brought them from the kitchen in two wooden dishes, and placed on the Floor, then they commenced eating it with their Fingers, and thus continued the performance till about ten o'clock when the Chief Elder desired the

---

accurate description of their songs, dances, marches, visits to the spirit land, etc., p. 16. Boston, 1850. Compare the "golden trumpet" song with the following:

> I am a little bird, I sing complete,
> Time the tune with my little feet,
> I can dance, and I can hop,
> I can shout and wake you up—

reported by Lamson about the same period. Lamson, David. Two years' experience among the Shakers. West Boylston (Mass.), 1848.

[49] The Shakers believed that the souls of the dead wandered about until they were converted and entered the Shaker heaven, a celestial community of stately spiritual buildings, gardens of delicious fruits and beautiful trees and flowers. The spirits of departed Believers held intimate communion with mortals who were already traveling the way of regeneration or resurrection. Through such psychic attunement, heavenly songs, melodies and messages could be imparted, and sensitive Shaker instruments could in turn envisage, and hear the voices of, the heavenly saints.

Indians to go away, and they would find some one waiting, to conduct them to the Shakers in the Heavenly world. At this announcement every man and woman became themselves again. . . .[50]

When the Eskimo spirits took possession of the bodies of brethren and sisters, the latter would perform the actions of driving dog-sledges: "they would move about the floor, give a whistle, and accompany it with a motion of the hand, as though they were flourishing a whip."[51] "Laplanders" and "Greenlanders" exercised themselves by "skating" about the floor; "melancholy Siberians" walked about with folded arms; "Arabs" sometimes seized and tried to hide various articles which they could lay their hands on; and "Abyssinians" jumped about boisteriously with loud frantic shouts. Included in these strange visitations were the spirits of Mexicans, Peruvians, Patagonians, Hottentots, Grecians, Persians, Turks, Moors, Chinese, Loo-choo Islanders, Jews and persons or families of Scotch, Irish, French and Spanish descent. The Indian, Negro and other racial songs sprang from the fantastic exercises attendant on these manifestations.[52]

In contrast to the Indian, Eskimo and other racial impersonations[53] were the rituals of purification, humility and mortification. The latter were deliberately organized, and the songs which accompanied them—"Scour and scrub," "Sweep sweep and cleanse your floor," "Step by inches," "The voice of God," "Cleanse your sanctuary," etc.—had a formal solemnity lacking in the "racial" songs. The first protracted ritual of the period, the "cleansing gift to purify all habitations," preceded the long-awaited visit of Holy Mother Wisdom on Christmas, 1841. For weeks much time had been spent in kneeling, silent prayer,

[50] Macdonald, A. J. Manuscript in Yale University library. Macdonald was a poor Scotch printer who came to this country in search of work and data on American social experiments. After his death his papers were found by John Humphrey Noyes, who used parts of the MS. in his "History of American Socialisms." (Philadelphia, 1870.)

The singing and dancing of the early Union Village Shakers reminded the Rev. Jonathan Leslie of what he had frequently seen practised by the Indians. "At certain turns in the music (he wrote) they spat on their hands, turned entirely round and still continued dancing. . . . (Leslie, Rev. Jonathan. The Shakers. From the Pittsburgh [Pa.] Recorder. In Niles' Register, Sept. 21, 1822.)

[51] A Return of Departed Spirits of the Highest Characters of Distinction, as well as the indiscriminate of all nations, into the bodies of the "Shakers," etc., p. 37. By an associate of said society. Philadelphia, 1843.

[52] See pp. 69-76, also songs 42-50.

[53] "A phase of Spiritualism directly opposite from that of the Indians was the manifestation of the Shepherdess." According to Elder Blinn, (op. cit., pp. 45-46) "she was a keeper of sheep, in her earth home, and represented herself as engaged in the same occupations since passing to the spirit land." Many songs were received from the Shepherdess in January and February, 1844. (See p. 69 and song No. 64.)

exhortations and warnings. Once a day, for six days before the event, the only food had been bread and water. Then, in conformity with a sacred writing called the Judgment Law, the "yearly sacrifice" or "opening of the mind" was held, followed by the above ritual. In this strange ceremony, a chosen band of instruments and singers marched through the dwellings and out-buildings, singing a song of vengeance ("The Voice of God"[54]) "against the abominations that had rested in Zion," and sweeping and cleaning (in pantomime) everywhere. Returning to the place of worship, all fell on their knees "to scour and scrub from this floor the stains of sin."[55]

"The Midnight Cry" was one of several ceremonials instituted in 1842, the year in which the revival, stimulated by the visitations of Wisdom, reached its climactic phases. Led by two mediums carrying lighted lamps, a company of six male and six female instruments marched through every room in every building, a work occupying nearly two weeks. At midnight on the third day, the family was aroused by four sisters who passed through the halls and sisters' retiring-rooms, singing

> Awake from your slumbers,
> For the Lord of Hosts is going through the land,
> He will sweep, he will clean his holy sanctuary.
> Search ye your Camps, yea read and understand,
> For the Lord of Hosts holds the Lamp in his hand.[56]

All members of the family then arose and joined the ranks. At two o'clock the next night the sleepers were again awakened by a company of brethren and sisters, and at three gathered in the meeting-room for an hour of worship. For eight years this ritual was enacted annually at New Lebanon, where it originated, and at Canterbury and other communities.

"Mother Ann's Sweeping Gift" was probably an outgrowth of "The Midnight Cry" and the "cleansing gift, and like the Cry, was performed once a year for eight years.[57] A communication from the foundress had directed that a day

---

[54] See Song No. 57. The "Voice of God" and other ritual songs belong in the same category as the "eccentric" songs of an earlier period. In the former ritual the brethren would roar and howl at the appropriate time, stamp their feet with the word "curse," and shake whenever they came upon any unclean spot.

[55] See Song No. 54.

[56] See Song No. 58. Several versions existed.

[57] The sweeping ritual may have originated in an episode at Watervliet a few days before Mother Ann died. As Hannah Goodrich, the first "mother" of the Canterbury-Enfield bishopric, was sweeping

be set aside for a general cleaning of houses, shops and premises—to remove those "evil spirits" which harbored themselves wherever there was dust or dirt. Accordingly, on the appointed day a band of instruments, preceded by a group of singers and the elders, marched through the community wielding "spiritual brooms" and chanting various sweeping, cleaning and "warring" songs. In the meantime the other members devoted themselves to the actual work of sweeping floors, dusting out cobwebs, picking up bits of wood and paper, burning rubbish, cleaning pig-pens, and placing everying in order until the village, already "notorious for neatness, wore an aspect fifty per cent more tidy than usual."

Songs played an important rôle in the elaborate ritualism of the mountain meetings (first instituted in 1842), as well as the Christmas ceremonials which began three years later.[58] A detailed account of the "feast days" on the holy hills would lead us afield, but the background for a number of ritual songs and dances should at least be sketched. Brief reference should also be made to two other phenomena of the great revival, the spiritual messages received by the instruments and the so-called inspirational drawings.

Word went forth from the New Lebanon ministry in 1842 that each society should select a hill or mountain top as a site for special semi-annual observances. These sacred feast-grounds, about a half-acre in area, were cleared, leveled and enclosed; an inner hexagonal plot known as the "fountain" was surrounded by a low fence and marked at one end by an appropriately-inscribed marble tablet. About the same time the Shaker societies and holy mounts were given spiritual names.[59]

---

the piazza floor, the prophetess came out and said, "Sweep clean." "I will, Mother," replied Hannah. Again Ann said, "Ah, sweep clean I say." And when Hannah again promised, the sick woman repeated her words: "But, I say, sweep clean." Then the young convert "perceived that Mother had reference to the floor of the heart." (Testimonies of the Life, Character, Revelations and Doctrines of our ever blessed Mother Ann Lee, etc., p. 332. Hancock, 1816.)

[58] Thanksgiving and Mother Ann's birthday (Feb. 29 or March 1) were also commemorated, but not with unusual services. For many years the 6th of August (the day Ann landed in America) was observed by a smoking meeting, when sisters as well as brethren united in the curious "gift." The children were supplied with herbs to smoke. (See Haskett, op. cit.; also Arfwedson, C. D. The United States and Canada, 1832-34. London, 1834.)

[59] New Lebanon, for instance, was called Holy Mount; Watervliet, Wisdom's Valley; Hancock, City of Peace; Tyringham, City of Love; Enfield (Conn.), City of Union; Harvard, Lovely Vineyard; Shirley, Pleasant Garden; Canterbury, Holy Ground; Enfield (N. H.), Chosen Vale; Alfred, Holy Land; Sabbathday Lake or New Gloucester, Chosen Land. The western societies also had spiritual

On the evening before the May and September feast-days the members of each Shaker family assembled, and in the dim candlelight of the meeting-room, received the heavenly garments designed for the occasion. As a double file of brethren at one end of the room, and of sisters at the other, slowly approached and kneeled in turn, the elders and eldresses took spiritual robes and dresses out of an imaginary chest, and in solemn pantomime presented them to the suppliant members. Ministering angels were present to clothe the brethren and sisters, who returned their thanks "in 4 low bows." The next morning, so arrayed, the members met at the Church and marched two abreast up the appointed hill.

The festivals at Hancock in 1842 were typical of what took place in all the societies.[60] Here "the shining company" broke their march at a half-way point called the Walnut Grove, where they gathered in a circle and received blessings, gifts and instructions from the instruments. As the worshippers approached the consecrated ground—called Mount Sinai at Hancock—a selected group of singers struck up the worded march:

> To Mount Sinai we are going
> With our voices sounding shrill,
> And our hearts unite in praises
> While we mount this holy hill.

After the instruments had been consecrated with "sweet incense" from spiritual "censors" and had received their "mantles of strength," a female medium passed around the fountain singing a song of blessing:

> I am a pretty dove
> Just come from above
> With holy holy mother's love and blessing
> I will feed you with crumbs
> That will satisfy your souls
> And give you strength and power.

---

designations. The feast grounds at New Lebanon were called Holy Mount; at Tyringham, Mount Horeb; at Enfield (Conn.), the Mount of Olives; at Harvard, Holy Hill of Zion; at Canterbury, Pleasant Grove; at Enfield (N. H.), Mount Assurance; at Union Village, Jehovah's Chosen Square; at South Union, The Holy Fountain of the Lord Jehovah; at Whitewater, Chosen Square.

[60] The ensuing account is based on a manuscript entitled "A Record Kept of the Several Meetings held Upon Mount Sinai by the Family Orders on Days of the Feasts." Hancock, beginning in 1842.

The ceremony opened with a lively dance in which everyone acted independently: shouting, clapping their hands, bowing low, turning, reeling, staggering, leaping, skipping and rolling upon the ground. Then followed a series of rituals, interrupted by the reception of spiritual gifts, more dances, prophetic utterances by the instruments, and many songs.

The first rite consisted of placing "two large white tubs," one for the brethren and one for the sisters, on either side of the fountain. In the ensuing pantomime, dippers and baskets of sponges were placed near the tubs; these were filled from the "fountain;" and when all was ready for bathing, the sisters and brethren on separate sides of the enclosure went through the motions of scrubbing each other clean. It was probably for use in such ceremonials that many of the cleansing and bathing songs were composed.

A curious mortification or humility rite followed the drinking of spiritual wine. The draught made all quite "merry," and an instrument shouted: "I feel just about right to sing the fool song." Then all joined in the following verse:

Come, come
Who will be a fool,
I will be a fool—[61]

at the same time "throwing fool" to each other, catching it, and acting as foolishly as possible.[62]

In the excitement of worship and the reception of gifts, many songs were sung extemporaneously. Indian spirits came to the meetings, and entering the bodies of the instruments, sang and danced native songs composed at the moment. In one part of the meeting the spirit of George Washington brought a box of spiritual guns for the brethren and a basket of musical instruments for the sisters; and while the former were "fireing" (sic) their guns, the latter played "lively and pleasant airs."

The sowing of spiritual seed from baskets slung over the arm was a common gift both on the mountains and in the community fields. This was done with a rhythmic cadence which made of the ritual a sort of dance. After the seed of blessing was sown the company passed over the ground again, sprinkling it

[61] Cf. the Shaker "drinking" songs, pp. 63-64, also songs 51-52.

[62] In a mortification rite witnessed by an anonymous observer during this period, "the inspired commence(d) with slapping their hands against their sides, and crowing in imitation of the barnyard fowl: —Some will cackle, others imitate the turkey,—duck—hen—goose, or guinea pig." (Extract from an unpublished manuscript on Shaker history, etc. Op. cit., p. 15.)

from "water-pots" which had been placed on their shoulders by the Saviour.

At Hancock the meetings culminated in an elaborate feast suggestive of the Lord's Supper or Eucharist. All kinds of spiritual food and fruit—apples, pears, peaches, pineapples, plums, cherries, apricots, grapes, berries, pomegranates, oranges, pies, sweet-cakes, bread and butter, locusts and wild honey, milk and honey, white wine and manna—were gathered from imaginary trees and gardens. These choice dainties were first served to the ministry and elders, who sat at a long spiritual table. After all were satisfied, an elder sang a song of blessing:

> Now I will bow low,
> Now I will bow low,
> Now I will bow low,
> Yea I will,
> That heavenly blessings
> My soul may fill.

Then, as the common members of the company were served, a holy angel "passed up and down the table," chanting: "can any soul murmer at the cross since by it the glory of heaven is added unto you. More zeal, more zeal, more zeal, more life, more fervency, more energy, more love, more thankfulness, more obedience, more strength, more power."

At the close of the festival, in the middle of the afternoon, the Believers marched four abreast from the hill-top, singing:

> I will march I will go
> In this pretty shining way,
> In freedom's lovely valley
> On my organ I will play.

Two songs which seem to have been sung chiefly at the mountain meetings were "The Savior's Universal Prayer" (the Lord's Prayer) and a piece which began, "And again, O heavenly Father, Hear Thy children's humble cry."

Comparable to the above ceremonials were the meetings held on Christmas by the separate family orders. This was an important day among the Shakers, the occasion for "perfect reconciliation," and the rites partook of an extreme pentecostal ardour. An instrument awakened the family at Hancock an hour earlier than usual by "sounding a gift song" through the halls of the communal dwelling. The march tune to which all filed into the meeting-room was one

FIG. 3.—A few copies of "Millennial Praises" bear the imprint "1812." The hymnal was one of two books issued by Talcott at the Hancock (Mass.) community.

FIG. 4.—The fine penmanship of Mary Hazzard made her one of the busiest scribes in the Shaker order. Many maps and several inspirational drawings are ascribed to this Church family eldress at New Lebanon. "Simple Gifts" appears in a number of eastern hymnals.

FIG. 5.—The text reads:

2nd Fam. Enfield

This song was sung and labored by the good
spirits as is here described Christmas eve
1853 and was seen and learned by Elder

Br Timothy R

In Shaker parlance it would be called a "noted song" since it is without words. The chart outlines the course of a file of marchers describing a series of circles.

FIG. 6.—Text of song:

Ho ho ho (Shout)
Now while my love is flowing
You are not forgotten;
You are mine, you are mine
My Sana Vince.

Come and share come and share
Of my love and blessing,
For with the faithful you shall have
A happy happy mansion.

Text within "leaf":

To my Sana Vince
This is golden leaf which
was gathered from the Tree of songs
Mother Lucy sends this by Elder
Sister Olive; with her kind love and
rememberance to Sister Molly B.—

Learned   Nov, 28th 1839
Thanksgiving day.

On the opposite side of the same hymnal page another leaf is outlined, with this enclosure:

Mother Lucy said
she thought it would please Molly
to receive this leaf, and be able
to see its form; and, how completely the song
borders the leaf. She says Molly likes
to see pretty things; and the
name of this leaf is,

E M B L E M.

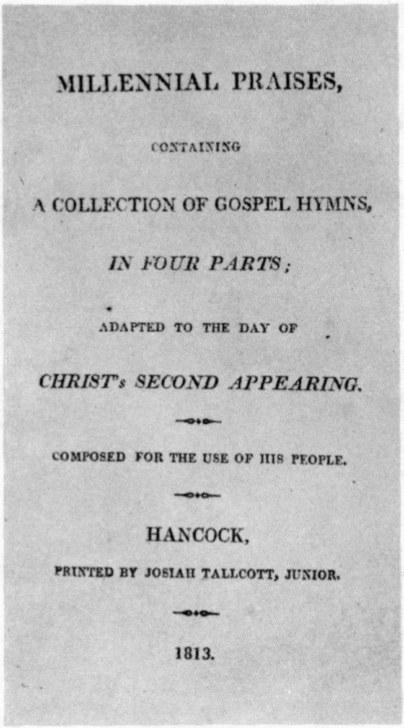

MILLENNIAL PRAISES,

CONTAINING

A COLLECTION OF GOSPEL HYMNS,

IN FOUR PARTS;

ADAPTED TO THE DAY OF

CHRIST's SECOND APPEARING.

COMPOSED FOR THE USE OF HIS PEOPLE.

HANCOCK,

PRINTED BY JOSIAH TALLCOTT, JUNIOR.

1813.

FIG. 3

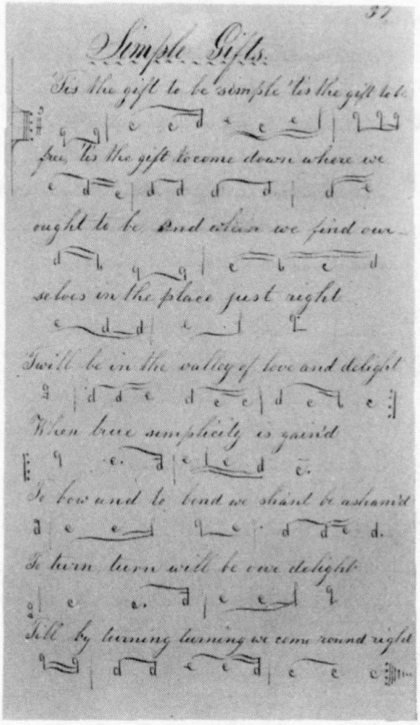

FIG. 4

Fig. 5

Fig. 6

"anciently sung and played upon instruments by the holy spirits on the day of Pentecost at the time the Apostles received the tongues of fire." The story of Christ's birth was simply told at the beginning of the meeting, during the course of which many spiritual presents—robes, shields, silver sacks, silver crosses, pitchers of never-failing water, bowls of fruit and celestial wine, etc.—were bestowed by the instruments acting in the name of the Holy Savior. At Hancock songs were sung as the worshippers sat on "carpets of Mother's love, soft as velvet." At Enfield, to the accompaniment of a solemn song called "The Sound," the exercise was "leaping up and down, and bringing our feet upon the floor with great energy of spirit, and keeping time with the song. When we came to the last sound, we suddenly came down upon our knees, beating the song with our hands upon the floor." [63]

At the Christmas meetings in the City of Union, sweeping songs such as the one which began—"My beauty, my union, my love, my love, my love, I will have love"—were sung to the rhythm of sweeping and brushing the meeting-rooms [64] with brooms received from the spirits. [65] At one of the meetings a "war song" was introduced by a message from one of the instruments—"Brethren and sisters, hate the flesh"—and by the distribution of spiritual swords. These were wielded in a lively manner as the following song was sung:

> Behold it is a time of war
> And we have been enlisting,
> Emmanuel we're fighting for
> And Satan we're resisting.
> We have not in this war begun
> To turn our backs as traitors
> But we will all unite as one
> Against our carnal natures.

The warring songs popular during the revival had their origin in early Shaker history. In the one quoted at the beginning of this chapter it was Mother, or the singer, who warred on evil. As early as 1782, however, Plumer (op. cit.)

[63] An account of the Meetings held in the City of Peace, City of Union, and City of Love, On the 25th of Dec. 1845. MS.

[64] See p. 32.

[65] Cf. work-songs of the southern negroes. There was no regimented labor among the Shakers and therefore no work-songs, only the "laboring" or exercise-songs of systematized worship. A song fragment from Canterbury—"Saluri-e, saluri-o, salurie in the work we go"—has been called a "work-song," an incorrect designation except as applied to *spiritual* work.

told how the Shakers sometimes gathered around a disbeliever stamping their feet and shouting, "Damn his devil, damn his devil!" In the warring gift reported by Lamson,[66] members crowded about a disobedient or faithless person shouting, shaking, stamping and crying "woe, woe, woe."

The act of chasing or shooting the devil was a revival ritual. In one account, as some one spies the devil coming into the meeting, he gives the alarm, whereupon every true believer "opens the battery at once." This was done "by drawing the right knee nearly to the chin, placing the arm in the position of a sportsman, then straightening themselves out with a jerk, and a stamp of the foot, accompanied by a quick bursting yelp, in imitation of a gun. . . ." As the devil starts to flee, cries arise: "See him dart!" "Shoot him!" "Kill him!" All rush for spiritual weapons from the "spiritual arsenal." The fight then commences.[67]

Such performances might be accentuated by such songs as

DISMISSION OF THE DEVIL

Be joyful, be joyful,
Be joyful, be joyful,
For Old Ugly is going.
Good ridance good riddance
Good ridance we say,
And don't you never come here again.

In the gift of the "Father and Son" and that of the "Father, Son and holy spirit," instruments possessed by these spirits marched up and down the assembled ranks in meeting, bestowing blessings and, by gently touching the head of each member with their hands, "crowning" each with the "seal" of divine "approbation." Sometimes the seal was received as the members prostrated themselves with their faces to the floor. For a week previous to the administration of this gift at Hancock, no worded songs were allowed in meeting, and only solemn marches. A similar rite was the "Gift of Holy Mother Wisdom," in which the instrument placed around the head of each bowing figure a golden band inscribed with Wisdom's name.

[66] Lamson, op. cit., p. 90.
[67] Extract from an unpublished manuscript on Shaker history, op. cit.

No account of the songs of the Believers would be complete without mention of the inspired messages and drawings produced during the great revival of 1837. Though few verses or pieces of music were included in these phenomenal documents, as further expressions of the same mystic afflatus they shed considerable light on the nature, origin and function of Shaker "gifts," and gift-songs in particular.

Hundreds of spiritual messages were received by chosen instruments in the 1840's from Mother Ann and other early leaders, the Heavenly Father and Holy Mother Wisdom, the Saviour, angels with resounding names, biblical saints and figures famous in history. Like the vision songs, these communications—composed chiefly of solemn warnings, prophecies, exhortations, injunctions and promises—were the product of dreams, trances, clair-audience or some psychic or mystic state of mind. Many messages, like many gift-songs, were addressed to particular persons in recognition of their faithfulness and good works, and as testimonials of such regard often included spiritual gifts: precious stones, balls of love, rods of comfort, chains of pure gold, silver bowls filled with Mother's love, fans of eternal truth, leaves from the tree of life, breastplates of wisdom, robes of meekness and purity, sweet-cakes, flowers, cups of wine, pipes "for smoking mothers love," and so on. Reference was sometimes made to a box or book of songs or a song brought on the wings of a dove; sometimes to singing birds, gospel trumpets, harps of love or holy musical instruments of God. Among the inspired gifts received by Albert Battles at Tyringham on Jan. 10, 1841 were a number of trumpets, with balls of love to put in them "so that when blown the messages of love will scatter." Occasionally an actual poem or song will be recorded in the manuscript books of messages, but as these books were never circulated it is unlikely that the songs were used in worship.

The long unrhymed anthems ("given by revelation and the gift of God,") which were set to music from about 1840 on, were closely related in spirit and content to the inspirational messages. Many were like prose poems which conformed, however, to no metrical pattern and could be sung only because Shaker notation allowed constant changes in mode, timing, barring or rhythm; others, written into the hymnals with no musical accompaniment, were probably chanted or recited if used in meeting at all. The most interesting were prophetic or mystic in character, reminding one of the strange revelations of the French Prophets. "Song of the East," an example of this type of anthem, was sent (with music) from Holy Wisdom by Mother Ann to Joanna Kitchel on April 21, 1844:

SONG OF THE EAST

Behold a plant springeth up in the east which shall heal many nations; this plant
saith Wisdom was by my own hand planted.

And a lamp goeth out of the wilderness which shall kindle a great burning.

France is my lamp, and England my plant, saith the Lord;

Spain is my defence, and Ireland my strength,

Germany my word, and Italy my sword.

I will make war with the nations of the earth,

I will scatter them in my fury and divide them in the four winds;

 and I will build me an house, a high house;

 no man can tell how I shall frame my house;

 but I will bring my timbers from afar a strange land

 and I will build my house in the east

 and many people shall flow into it.

And my household shall be in ev'ry land;

 and they shall subdue all nations.

Then my name shall be glorified by Priests and Kings

 and all the earth shall tremble before me,

 for I alone will be exalted in that day saith God,

 and here my word doth end.

Now arise and prepare the way for my people,

O daughter of the East that when I come again,

I may visit thee in mercy.

"Learn of Me the Saviour," given here only in part, promises a reward for
good works:

Arise in peace and follow me for I am your Savior—with a gentle voice I call
every one both great & small to come come learn to be meek & lowly learn learn
that blessed are the poor in spirit who delight to do their heavenly Father's will.
Tho bread should fail & fountains dry their garners I will fill. . . .

"A Prayer for the Needy," another type of long anthem, begins:

O Righteous holy Father lend a listning ear unto our hunble cry. O Yea we do
bow in true supplication before thee O Lord and humbly implore thy mercy in
behalf of the poor and needy souls that are groping in darkness and have strayed far
far away from thee. . . .

The inspirational or emblematic drawings produced in the period between 1844 and 1859 were really messages in pictorial form. The designers of these symbolic documents felt that their work was controlled by supernatural agencies, sometimes the spirit of a departed Shaker saint, and that like the songs they were thus gifts from above—gifts bestowed on some individual in the order (usually not the one who made the drawing) as a reward of merit or token of regard. The designs might be called visionary drawings, for like the songs again, they were inspired by dreams or visions of the beauty of paradise, "the heavenly sphere." In them were pictured union or order; celestial bowers; tables of spiritual food; heavenly fruits, exotic flowers and rare plants, angels and saints; birds carrying messages, golden chariots, beautiful mansions, bright burning lamps; and many biblical objects literally or imaginatively rendered.[68]

The drawings (which were done both in color and black or blue ink) often contained poems inscribed in a circle, heart or perhaps a scroll carried by a dove or angel, but such verses were never set to music or sung in meeting. From the viewpoint of Shaker song, the most interesting aspect of the designs were the musical instruments which often were pictured: golden harps, bugles, trumpets, horns, drums, "dulcimers of music," clarions, cages of "spiritual singing birds," an elaborate "musical machine," "an instrument of heavenly music," etc. Instrumental music, it appears, was welcome in the world above. Like the heavenly robes, the delicious food, the precious stones and ornamental buildings, they were rewards for good works below, compensations for natural desires prohibited by Shaker law and custom. In the earth life, Mother Ann condemned steeple houses, costly furniture, slovenly ease, superfluous music—yet in a drawing of a "fruit-bearing tree" there is a golden chair where the prophetess was wont to sit and sing as her angels, playing on harps and "dulcimers of music," danced around her.

Distinct though they may be in textual content,[69] Shaker spirituals belong to the broad tradition of all religious folk-song. In gaiety of spirit, in rhythm, often

[68] Cf. Wilkinson, W. S. Spirit Drawings: A Personal Narrative. London, 1858. The drawings described by Wilkinson were the product of a primitive "mental vision," "a new faculty of the mind," a sixth sense, and above all, a faith that such "gifts" were possible. The subjects were often similar to those drawn by the Shakers: mansions of the soul, fountains, lamps (the "external conscience"), symbolic trees, flowers of love, joy, humility, etc.

[69] Occasionally one will happen on a Shaker song with a non-Shaker text. "The Saviour's Universal Prayer," for instance, which was sung at the mountain meetings at Hancock, was an unaltered version of the Lord's Prayer. "Followers of the Lamb" is closely related to "My Bible Leads to Glory."

in structure (in the use of repetition, for example) the lively Shaker pieces suggest the game songs of children, the play-party songs of early America, the exuberance and spontaneous utterances of the young in heart everywhere. In spite of their insular pride and defensive attitude towards worldly things, the Believers were not averse to borrowing from the outside; nor could they, if they would, completely cut themselves off from the denominational influences of their pre-Shaker lives.

The songs in unknown tongues, for instance, were not unlike the "counting out" songs, the nonsense rhymes and jargon which children of the world, to see who was "it," would recite or sing with gay abandonment. An example is

> Eeney, meeny, tip te te,
> Teena, Dinah, Domine. . . .

"All that" is modeled on Robert Burns' "'A' That." Prof. George Pullen Jackson has noted the similarity in text between the Shakers' "Pure Gospel" and the down-east spiritual, "True Happiness." Compare also the old Shaker hymn, "Adieu Earthly Pleasure," with the Mormon "Farewell Earthly Honor."

A song rendered ("with appropriate gestures") by two Canterbury sisters while on a visit to Bridgewater, N. H. in 1857 starts thus:

> I put my right hand in, I put my right hand out;
> I give my right hand a shake, shake, shake and I
> turn myself about.

As the song continues, the "left hand" is put in, then the "right foot," then the "left foot," then "my whole head."

Mr. Phillips Barry has pointed out that this was known as a children's game, the oldest printed version of which was called "Hinkum-booby." (P. B. and Henry, Mellinger E. Shaker Songs and Music. In Bulletin of the Folk-Song Society of the Northeast, No. 4, pp. 17-18. Cambridge, 1932. Also R. Chambers, Popular Rhymes of Scotland. Edinburgh, 1842, p. 65.) Lady Gomme (Traditional Games, I) referred to certain British versions as a "sacred dance" in which the performers spun round and round. Newell gave it the title, "Right Elbow In," and said that it was danced "deliberately and decorously . . . with slow rhythmical motion." (Newell, William Wells. Games and Songs of American Children, p. 131. New York, 1883.) Newell's version was

> Put your right elbow in,
> Put your right elbow out,
> Shake yourselves a little,
> And turn yourselves about.

Then follow "left elbow," "right ear," "left ear," "right foot," "left foot," etc.

It is possible, of course, that a convert brought the song to Canterbury, where it was adapted to a dance or ritual; the words and motions of shaking would have made it popular, though it does not seem to have been much used in the Shaker societies.

[42]

which may be compared to the Shaker

> E ne me ne mo del e
> Sane to luro lu ral lee . . .

A counting rhyme quoted by Newell,

> Onery, uery, ickery, see
> Huckabone, crackabone, tillibonee;
> Ram pang, muski dan,
> Striddle dum, straddledum, twenty one . . .

has the same essential form and spirit as the following Shaker "Indian" tune:

> Hock a nick a hick nick
> Qwine qui quo cum
> Jac a ling shack a ling
> Hick a chick a loreum.

Many such comparisons might be cited. In this connection, it is an interesting fact that children in sections where there were Shaker villages were wont to recite, as nonsense verses or tongue-twisters, songs which were indubitably of Shaker origin.

The repetition of lines, phrases or words is also characteristic of children's game songs. The compositions of the Believers were written for simple rounds and forward-and-backward movements which remind one of kindergarten exercises. In certain numbers, like "Vive Vum," a single line may be sung over and over again; in others, words like "shake," "low" or "love" may be repeated several times to accent a gesture or mood. The recurrent lines in "Mothers Golden Trumpet," "Take my hands," "Followers of the Lamb," "Be Joyful," "A handful of gospel love," "O my mother's wine," "Shake shake shake in the valley low," "Come mother's love," etc., illustrate a tendency also existent in nursery rhymes and play songs. In another type of Shaker song the Believers, again in the manner of children, spelled out the letters of certain words, sometimes going through a whole piece in this way. In the hymnals the letters of such words were dotted underneath—as in "Love and Blessing"[70] (1839), which

---

[70] See song No. 69.

was first spelled out and then sung (with a change in the melody) in the usual way:

> mother   sends   her   love   and
>   blessing
> to   comfort   and   strengthen   all.

The ideas and imagery of many Shaker songs, and the conduct of the worshippers as they voiced these ideas, constantly remind one of the ways of children and "simple folk." They receive such "simple little gifts" as pretty drums, balls of simplicity, pretty rings, a little plum cake or a sweet pudding.[71] They imagine that they are little birds singing, or little busy bees. They hear Mother tooting her trumpet; they receive from her permission to play. They toss balls of love to one another and "hop up and jump up" to catch imaginary gifts. Sometimes they just act silly, as in the fool song. The laughing and turning songs have their counterpart in many children's games; the "Indian," "Eskimo" and other racial songs and antics are the expression of children "making believe." Many "gifts" and rituals—chasing the devil out of the room, scrubbing one another with "sponges," sowing seed, pretending to eat luscious fruits, making the motions of playing on trumpets, etc.—were essentially games.

The Shakers took pride, in fact, in being "Mother's little children," "Mother's little lambs," "Children of the free Woman," etc., and after their exercises in the meeting-house spoke of their worship as a "joyful" time or "merry frolick." It was, indeed, a return to a state of innocence or unrestrained primitivism—a recreation in which their souls were uplifted and sustained. Over the meeting-house door might well have been written the Saviour's precept: "Except ye . . . become as little children, ye shall not enter into the kingdom of heaven."

Though worship reached its most fantastic extremes between 1842 and 1845, when the sabbath meetings were closed to the world, and though most of the "spirits," particularly those who made actual visitations, took their "departure" about 1847, there was little abatement, throughout the 1840's, in the outpouring of songs and spiritual "notices." Throughout the decade hundreds of changes were rung on the themes of gospel love, union, "freedom from bondage," and above all, meekness or humility. Each song was prized as a precious jewel, a pure and sacred token sent directly from the heavens as a mark of God's ap-

---

[71] See "I have a little drum" (song 41), "I have a little union bell" (song 22), etc., which are built on a genuine folk pattern.

probation. No wonder that the law-makers of the sect, jealous lest these spiritual gifts be "naturalized," forbade brethren and sisters from learning them in each others' shops or rooms.

By 1850, however, it was evident that the tide of mysticism was beginning to ebb.[72] Songs in the fifties and sixties were still attributed to spirits, exchanged as gifts and copied into manuscript hymnals. But in these later compositions, as in other forms of expression, the exuberance of the early stages of the revival is less and less evident. Now and again an original song or characteristic tune would make its appearance. Sometimes the Shaker meeting itself would revert to the fervent formlessness of an earlier period. In the main, however, the various forms of worship assumed a more and more imitative, repetitious character. The songs printed in "The Shaker," a monthly which began publication in 1871, were strictly orthodox in content and set to the round notes and five-line staff of worldly music.[73]

Two closely related questions, not easily answered, arise in connection with the hundreds of songs produced during the great revival. First, under just what circumstances were the vision and gift songs, tunes and words alike, received? Secondly, how could the transcriber or score-pricker remember the whole song after hearing the communicant sing it but once?

As regards the first query, it should be noted that the earliest vision songs were brief utterances, readily recalled and immediately written down as a religious duty. If these "songs" were sung in a state of trance, dream or ecstasy, it is difficult to believe that they would follow a tonal or metrical pattern, or that the pieces could have been fully recorded by the same person after the reception of the "gift." The piecing out of the text with repeated words and melodic phrases indicates after-construction on somebody's part.

The longer gift songs were also said to have originated in spiritual realms, being sent directly to some instrument by Mother Ann or other saints. Here again we encounter the difficulty of reconciling a fantastic "visionary" experience with the neat, scientific song-renderings in the manuscript hymnals. In the

[72] Many Shakers believed that the spirits left their communities to manifest themselves to the world. For it was in the year 1848 that the Fox sisters in Hydesville, N. Y., first heard the mysterious rappings which ushered in modern spiritualism.

[73] In 1870, on the suggestion of Prof. B. B. Davis of Concord, N. H. and Dr. C. A. Guilmette of Boston, classes in the theory and practice of vocal music were established at the Canterbury community. In November of that year a melodeon was purchased, and two years later a piano. An example of the leaflet-songs distributed at Canterbury after 1870 is shown in Fig. 13.

absence of any evidence as to what took place when a visionist received a message, symbolic present or song, it would be hazardous to analyze the psychic processes involved. The statement can be ventured, however, that the instruments were acutely sensitive to the forces of the afflatus; and that they either dreamed, imagined or *felt* that these various gifts emanated from such and such a spirit. As the "lead" pronounced them to be genuine manifestations, flattered the instruments by calling them "God's Holy Anointed Ones," etc., and ordered all revelations to be recorded, it was natural that inspirational songwriting should have been stimulated. The *elements* of the song were undoubtedly produced by the visionist—though we can be fairly certain that in many cases the piece was reshaped, improved, titled and properly notated by another, a deliberate and experienced hand.

It is also unlikely that a worshipper who spontaneously sang a "song" in the excitement of worship would be able to remember it afterwards. Many songs, as well as many messages and the visionary experiences which resulted in the inspirational drawings, also were recorded days or weeks after the event. Tunes were fitted to words, and words to tunes. If the visionist had the ability, especially a knowledge of music, to make the record herself or himself, no assistance was required: but in many cases the gifts were recorded by versifiers like Mary Hazzard, Henry DeWitt, Russel Haskell, Isaac Youngs, D. A. Buckingham and others familiar with the rules of melody. The completed tune-and-text was built up into acceptable form from the unorganized elements of the original inspirational experience. These observations supply the answer to our second question.

Any one familiar with the singing, in their native milieu, of American folksongs, knows how freely these songs are rendered: the actual singing is based on but not necessarily confined to the song's skeletonic structure. The writer was first made aware of this point when he asked an aged Shakeress—Sister Sarah Collins of the Second family, New Lebanon—to sing " 'Tis the Gift to be Simple." The rhythm was there, the spirit of the song, most of the words, the *feeling* of the tune. But even when allowance was made for voice-decline, it could be seen what liberties she took with the melody as it appeared in the manuscript hymnal. The tune was twisted, there were unexpected flips and slurs—but the song emerged as a vibrant, living thing.

In spite of the singing-meetings, the preparation given each number in retiring-time, and the insistence on order and discipline, the songs of the Believers would often transcend their recorded forms. The frequent appoggiaturas before (and sometimes after) a note were symbols of an unrestrained elaboration of the melody—the only marks the score-pricker could give of a wild abandonment, the reaching for one note after another. A staccato may be a "mark of distinction" or a triumphant shout. Where there is a sign of repetition, the tune may have been repeated once or a dozen times. A trill might mean a great emotional trembling of voices. All the songs of the sect should be viewed as choral numbers, with emotion and ritualistic implications constantly influencing the rendering of the song.

A COLLECTION OF TEXTS ILLUSTRATING VARIOUS TYPES OF SHAKER SONGS [74]

    1. Hymns and anthems
    2. Dance songs
    3. Ritualistic and gestural songs
    4. Songs accompanied by spiritual presents
    5. "Indian" songs
    6. "Negro" songs
    7. Songs in unknown tongues
    8. Vision songs
    9. Vision songs (wholly or partly in unknown tongues)
   10. Songs of humility ("low" songs)

1. Hymns and anthems

MOTHER [75]

    1. Let names and sects and parties
       Accost my ears no more,
       My ever blessed Mother,
       Forever I'll adore:
       Appointed by kind heaven,
       My Saviour to reveal,
       Her doctrine is confirmed
       With an eternal seal.

[74] In the original manuscript hymnals, most of these songs had tune-accompaniments. Except for the hymns and anthems, which were not usually dance or exercise songs, the grouping is overlapping and somewhat arbitrary. Thus, a dance song may involve shaking, bowing, turning, "reeling" or other bodily "exercise." Gift songs in which spiritual gifts or presents were received may likewise have been sung with gestures or movements akin to a dance; sometimes vision songs were called

2. She was the Lords anointed,
   To show the root of sin;
   And in its full destruction,
   Her gospel did begin:
   She strip'd a carnal nature,
   Of all its deep disguise,
   And laid it plain and naked,
   Before the sinner's eyes.

3. "Sunk in your base corruptions,
   Ye wicked and unclean!
   You read your sealed Bibles,
   But know not what they mean:
   Confess your filthy actions,
   And put your lusts away,
   And live the life of Jesus;
   This is the only way.

4. Ye haughty kings and beggars,
   Come learn your equal fate!
   Your carnal fallen natures,
   You all must surely hate:
   Whatever your profession,
   Your sex or colour be,
   Renounce your carnal pleasures,
   Or Christ you'll never see.

5. The way of God is holy,
   Mark'd with Immanuel's feet;
   Lust cannot reach mount Zion,
   Nor stain the golden street.
   If you will have salvation,
   You first must count the cost,
   And sacrifice that nature,
   In which the world is lost."

gift songs because the words or tunes were "given" in a vision. Racial and vision songs were some-times rendered, in whole or in part, in "unknown" or "strange" tongues. Classification is based on the chief characteristic or purpose of the song. Texts recorded verbatim from original MSS.

75 From Millennial Praises, Part II, Hymn 11, pp. 78-82. Said to have been written by Elder Richard McNemar of the Union Village community.

6. At Manchester, in England,
This blessed fire began,
And like a flame in stubble,
From house to house it ran:
A few at first receiv'd it,
And did their lusts forsake;
And soon their inward power
Brought on a mighty shake.

7. The rulers cried, "Delusion!
Who can these Shakers be?
Are these the wild fanatics,
Bewitched by Ann Lee?
We'll stop this noise and shaking,
It never shall prevail;
We'll seize the grand deceiver,
And thrust her into jail."

8. Before their learned councils,
Though oft she was arraign'd,
Her life was uncondemned,
Her character unstain'd:
And by her painful travel,
Her suff'rings and her toil,
A little Church was formed
On the European soil.

9. This little band of union,
In apostolic life,
Remain'd awhile in England,
Among the sons of strife;
Till the Columbian Eagle,
Borne by an eastern breeze,
Convey'd this little Kingdom
Across the rolling Seas.

[49]

10. To mark their shining passage,
    Good angels flew before,
    Towards the land of promise,
    Columbia's happy shore.
    Hail, thou victorious gospel!
    And that auspicious day,
    When Mother safely landed
    In Hudson's lovely bay!

11. Near Albany they settled,
    And waited for a while,
    Until a mighty shaking
    Made all the desert smile.
    At length a gentle whisper,
    The tidings did convey,
    And many flock'd to Mother,
    To learn the living way.

12. Through storms of persecution,
    The truth she did maintain,
    And show'd how sin was conquer'd,
    And how we're born again:
    The old corrupted nature,
    From place to place she trod,
    And show'd a new creation,
    The only way of God.

13. About four years she labour'd
    With the attentive throng,
    Confirm'd the young believers,
    And help'd their souls along.
    At length she clos'd her labour,
    And vanish'd out of sight,
    And left the Church increasing,
    In the pure gospel light.

14. How much are they deceived,
    Who think that Mother's dead!
    She lives among her offspring,
    Who just begin to spread;
    And in her outward order,
    There's one supplies her room,
    And still the name of Mother,
    Is like a sweet perfume.

15. Since Mother sent the gospel,
    And spread it in the west,
    How many sons and daughters
    Are nourish'd from her breast!
    How many more conceived,
    And trav'ling in the birth!
    Who yet shall reign with Mother,
    Like princes on the earth.

16. I love that testimony,
    That shows me what to do;
    I love my precious Mother,
    I love the Elders too;
    The Brethren and the Sisters,
    I love them and their ways,
    And in this loving spirit,
    I mean to spend my days.

A HYMN OF LOVE

Love the inward, new creation,
Love the glory that it brings;
Love to lay a good foundation,
In the line of outward things.
Love a life of true devotion,
Love your lead in outward care;
Love to see all hands in motion,
Love to take your equal share.

Love to love what is belov'd,
Love to hate what is abhorr'd;
Love all earnest souls that covet
Lovely love and its reward.
Love repays the lovely lover,
And in lovely ranks above,
Lovely love shall live for ever,
Loving lovely loved love.[76]

ALL THAT [77]

1. Tho many foes beset me round
   My self and pride and all that
   Yet since the way of life I've found
   I'll bear my cross for all that
   For all that and all that
   My hatred strife and all that
   The noble soul that's truly wise
   Will trample soon on all that.

2. Tho satan comes with iron bands
   To bind my soul and all that
   I'll vengeance sweare with lifted hands
   I will be free for all that
   For all that and all that
   Tho devils rage and all that
   Obedience and simplicity
   Will conquer hell for all that.

3. Tho many trials daily rise
   Unseen before and all that
   Yet they who still have open eyes
   Will see it right for all that
   For all that and all that
   They stumble not at all that
   In order self to crucify
   They feel the need of all that.

[76] Fragment of "A Hymn of Love" published by Thomas Brown in his account of the Shakers, 1812. With the exception of the last line, which in "Millennial Praises" reads "Loving with eternal

Fig. 7.—For a description of the mountain meetings. The house in the background is a shelter. At the head of the "fountain" stand the ministry, the leading elders and eldresses of the community or bishopric.

FIG. 8.—This drawing, unsigned, appeared in Frank Leslie's Popular Monthly, December, 1885, as an illustration for an article on "The Shakers in Niskayuna." Because it was credited in another printing to Joseph Becker, we suspect that the other Leslie drawings, notably the religious dance in Fig. 16, were the work of the same artist.

4. Yet hypocrits within may creep
And think their hid and all that
A wolf cannot become a sheep
Because they'r here for all that
For all that and all that
Their saintish looks and all that
They will be turne'd inside out
And be a-shimed of all that.

THE ROCK [78]

1. I want to feel little
I want to feel small
The last of my Brethren
The least of them all
Chorus: That I may inherit
That pure gospel spirit
The spirit of Christ
And of Mother.

2. I want to feel humble
And simple in mind
More watchful more careful
More fully resigned
Chorus: That I may inherit, etc.

3. I want to be holy
More perfect in love
I want to be gentle
And meek as a dove
Chorus: That I may inherit, etc.

Love," it is the same as Hymn XXVIII, Part II ("Love") in the Shaker hymnal. Communal love found formal expression in daily relationships as well as in song: when Believers met each other in the early years of the order, their greeting was always "More love, brother," or "More love, sister."

[77] From "A Collection of Hymns, and Spiritual Songs, Improved in our General worship. New Lebanon. November The 27th 1830." (MS. 102) A parody of Robert Burns' "A' That."

[78] Early hymn of humility. (From "A Collection of Hymns, Selected from diferent parts. Improved in our General Worship. Written by Elizabeth Lovegrove. 1822." New Lebanon. MS. 101.)

4. I want to be subject
   Unto every gift
   That when the rest travil
   I may not be left
Chorus: Then I shall inherit
   That pure gospel spirit
   The spirit of Christ
   And of Mother.

———————

O I will be a living soul and free from all that's evil.
Yea I will.
I'll hate the crooked winding paths that lead unto the devil.
Yea I do.
I'll turn away from evil, I'll turn away from strife,
I ever will be joined unto the tree of life.
Yea I will. . . .

Early Sabbathday Lake hymn, with chorus.

2. *Dance Songs.*

Come, Sister, come,
Lets all be one,
For you're as good as I am,
There is no cause
For picking flaws
For we're all going to Zion.

Unknown Origin.

Cross cross ev'ry one
Cross a carnal nature
Cross cross ev'ry one
And be a just partaker.

Lucy Gates. New Lebanon? March 27, 1838.

[54]

Awake my soul arise and shake
No time to ever ponder
Keep awake keep awake
Lest ye be rent assunder
I will be good I will be free,
I'll hate the old deceiver,
No earthly tie shall fetter me,
I'll be a good believer.

> *From the western Shakers, n.d. Compare this and
> other songs with the many contemporaneous or
> earlier non-Shaker hymns beginning with the word
> "awake:" "Awake my heart, arise my tongue,"
> "Awake our souls, away our fears," "Awake my
> soul to joyous days," etc.*

I want freedom I want love
I want the pretty gifts that come from above
I hate bondage & I'll not be bound
Come pretty freedom & love flow around.

> *Shirley, n.d.*

I want I want more love,
Mother's love I want,
I want Mother's love measured,
Heap'd up, heap'd up,
Press'd down, press'd down.

> *Early dancing song. First Order.
> New Lebanon. 1839.*

Mother's love I want to feel
Father William's power
The innocence of Father James
O heaven on me shower.

> *Round dance. New Gloucester.
> Aug. 1856.*

WAKE UP

Wake up be alive
Step the tune with power
Zealous be to grow and thrive
Every day and hour
Shuffle solid firm and strong
Every motion limber
While you time the holy song
Of Zions chosen number.

Cynthia Annis, n.p., n.d.

I have a little simple song
I sing it as I jog along,
Jog along, jog along
I sing it as I jog along
One foot up the other down
Tread the serpent to the ground,
This the way I jog along,
Jog along, jog along.

Sabbathday Lake or Alfred, Maine, n.d.

I used to dance before the Lord
Which grieved Michael sorely
I'll dance and dance and dance again
Her pride shall never hold me.
I'll not be bound by any man
Nor yet by woman's fancies
I am a merry merry soul
I'm lively in the dances.

Unknown origin.

Come, let us all be marching on,
Into the New-Jerusalem:
The call is now to ev'ry one
To be alive and moving.
This precious call we will obey
We love to march the heavenly way
And in it we can dance and play,
And feel our spirits living.

An early march. Unknown origin.

I hate the Old deceiver
He is an unbeliever
I will have nothing to do
With the old deceiver.
And when he comes round
I will tell him leave the ground
Or the first he will know
He'll receive a heavy blow.

A march. Unknown origin.

Come be advancing,
Move while the waters move.
It is a day of healing,
The pool is in commotion.
Don't be a-waiting,
Mother's love is flowing,
She is inviting
And we will be going.

Early quick dance. First order. 1837.
New Lebanon.

QUICK DANCE

Leap and skip ye little band
Shaker faith will fill the land
O the comfort life and zeal
Little Shaker children feel
Shaking is the work of God
And it has to spread abroad
Till the wicked feel and know
God Almighty reigns below.

Sabbathday Lake hymnal. Song dated
April 15, 1849.

A MARCH

See the Angels all around us
    pouring out their sweetest love
Chorus: Bless the Lord I'm happy.
Holy Mother too is with us
    dont you feel her tender love.
Chorus: Bless the Lord I'm happy.

From a Maine MS., about 1847.

3. Ritualistic and gestural songs.[79]

Keep the fire a-burning
Keep the wheel a-turning
Never mind the squirming
Of the Old Deceiver.

He's got to feel the strong rack
He's got to stand a-w-a-y back
He cannot walk the pure track
Of a good Believer.

Unknown origin.

Sweep sweep & cleanse your floor
Mother's standing at the door,
She'll give us good & precious wheat,
With which there is no chaff nor cheat,
I'll sow my wheat upon the ground
That's plough'd & till'd & where is found
A faithful laborer of the field
That it a rich increase may yield.

Eleanor Potter's song. New Lebanon,
March 27, 1839.

---

[79] There were only a few set rituals—like Scour & Scrub, Cleanse Ye your camps, The Voice of God, The Narrow Path (Precept & Line), etc.—for which songs were composed. In many songs, however, the singers acted out their words or thought in similar but more irregular fashion. "Sweeping" songs and those attended by shaking, turning, bowing and reeling (as if intoxicated) may all be included in this same general category. Some though not all of such pieces have a rhythmic pace which made them suitable for dancing.

CHILDREN OF THE FREE WOMAN

We're children of the free woman,
We're free'd from the bondage of sin and death
If we have any bands a binding on us
We must break them and break them and burn them up.

Sung by Elder Br. John, Oct. 26,
1839, n.p.

O come Mother's little children,
Wake up wake up,
O come Mother's little children,
Wake up, keep the fire burning.
O let the fire burn,
Hotter the better,
O let the fire burn,
Burn up all thats evil.

Union Village, n.d.

DISMISSION OF THE DEVIL

Be joyful, be joyful,
Be joyful, be joyful,
For Old ugly is going.
Good ridance, good ridance,
Good ridance we say,
And don't you never come here again.

Unknown origin.

Like the little busy bee
I'll fly around and be so free,
I'll sip the honey from the hive
And this will make me all alive.

Unknown origin. Probably a round dance song.

THE SHAMEFUL THREE

Get away old cross
Get away old snup
Get away old shall from me
Shame O shame
Shame O shame
Shame on you.

> *Unknown origin. "Snup" probably means "snap."*
> *The burden of the song is, do not be cross, sharp-*
> *tongued or wilful.*

DECISIVE WORK

I have come,
And I've not come in vain.
I have come to sweep
The house of the Lord
Clean, clean, for I've come
And I've not come in vain.
With my broom in my hand,
With my fan and my flail,
This work I will do
And I will not fail,
For lo! I have come
And I've not come in vain.

> *Sung by the Saviour and Mother Ann. (New*
> *Lebanon?) Sat. eve. Feby 21st 1845.*

O now I mean to rise and fight,
Fight with vengeance.
Shake off the nasty flesh
With every other hinderance.
Go off & stay away,
O you old deceiver.
Now from you I will be free
And be a good Believer.

> *Union Village, 1848.*

Ho, ho I've been a-drinking out of Mothers good wine lunkin (?)
Lo it takes my every feeling, sets me turning, twisting, reeling,
See it takes my head in earnest, hands, feet too at its service,
Lo lo this wine of Mother makes both bone and muscle quiver.
Cramp and stiff it will dissolve them, bend you down again twill straighten,
Try it, try it, drink it hearty, it will give you joints a-plenty.

A "drinking" song from New Gloucester, n.d.

Now we will be united and brush off pride and stiff,
Come brush, yea brush and brush again till limber as a withe.
Lets' turn around and shake off and break away the bands,
Till we are free and simple enough to shake hands,
And now we'll unite in the dance and the song,
Come turn away from evil and all that is wrong,
Then O how happy we'll be
When from all evil we're perfectly free.

Maine hymnal. n.d.

Me take one two steps in the little narrow way
Me three four five six find the alle sele qua
Seven eight down down Nine ten further
Eleven twelve thirteen then me find Mother.

Probably a regional version of "The Narrow Path"
Sabbathday Lake or New Gloucester hymnal, n.d.

Can't you bend your necks a little just a little little little
Can't you bend your necks a little to receive Mothers love
Mother says tis not the haughty who can share my love so freely
But tis those who're truly simple who receive a full supply.

New Enfield (Enfield, N. H.) April, 1848.

I feel the gospel fire burning in my very soul
Tis kindled against old slug and old drawback
Who always will be on the trac
Begone I say begone I say, you shall not in my bosom coil
To rob the comforts of my soul.

Maine hymnal, n.d.

MOTHER'S GOLDEN TRUMPET

Hear ye, hear ye, hear ye the trumpet
    toot toot toot,
Its Mother's golden trumpet,
Its Mother's golden trumpet,
Its Mother's golden trumpet,
    toot toot toot.
Mother is calling, she's calling, calling her children
    toot toot toot,
She's calling, she's calling, calling her children
Under the banner of love.

From White Water. Learn'd of Archibald M.
June 1843.

AN INDIGNANT SHAKE

I hate my pride deceit and lust,
I'll war with them forever,
I know of God they are accurst,
And every good Believer.
No peace with them I'll ever make,
They (re) doomed to desolation,
Against them now I want to shake
Shake with Indignation.

A song of mortification. Unknown origin.

ITS TIME TO STIR YOURSELVES

Wake up wake up ye sleepy souls
And be alive and don't be dead,
There is no time to sleep I say,
Now in this great and glorious day.
Dont be sleeping there so sound,
Get up yourselves and stir around
For if you want to keep awake
Arise and give a mighty shake.

East (?) Order, N. H. (Enfield or Canterbury).
Nov. 18th 1850.

HOLY POWER

Ill shake off bondage,
   Ill shake off pride,
Ill shake off every band
Thats round me tied.
I want to turn
And twist and reel,
No matter how much
This power I feel.

Oct. 26th 1850—n.p.

O come young friends let us be good
So we may feast on angels' food.
We'll take a sup of Mother's wine
For more than half is love divine.
And if it sits us on the floor
Twill only make us simple,
Arise and take a little more,
And this will make us limber.

A "drinking" song of unknown origin and date.

Here is a little love a little love jump up and ketch it
This is the way that I did receive it
Turn around around ketch a little more
For this is the way that I gathered my store.

Sabbathday Lake hymnal, n.d.

Drink ye of Mother's wine,
Drink drink drink ye freely,
Drink ye of Mother's wine
It will make you limber.
If it makes you reel around,
If it makes you fall down
If it lays you on the floor
Rise and take a little more.

Unknown origin.

Come come turn away,
Twist a way from bondage,
No matter what means you use
This to accomplish.
Reel and stagger twist about,
Laugh a little ha, ha,
O it is a feeling good
To be from bondage far.

(New Lebanon?) Church. 1848.

LIMBER ZEAL

In my Mother's love I will bow, bow, bow,
I will shake every fetter from my soul as I go,
Never minding the shape nor the form I am in
If I am but conquering the nature of sin.
Let the gift come as twill I am ready to move,
To be twisted and turned any way in Mother's love.
For the freedom of the spirit is my motto you'll see,
And with this every motion shall fully agree.
Now in limber zeal I will twist and reel
And show how I feel full of Mother's love, love.
Trol ol de dum dadle dum dum da de
Trol ol de dum dadle dum dum dum dum.

*Sung by Br. Jack ("a colored spirit") in the
Church, Chosen Vale (Enfield, N. H.) 1848.*

O my Mothers wine I love it,
O my Mothers wine I love it,
O my mothers wine I love it,
It will make me stagger.
O it makes me feel so pretty,
O it makes me feel so low,
O it makes the devil hate me
When all evil has to go.

*Sent from Ohio to Betsy Bates by Nancy McNemar.
(Union Village, n.d.) Another "drinking" song.*

[64]

4. *Songs accompanied by spiritual presents.*[80]

Only look, look and see,
Pretty treasures given me.
One and two, three and four.
All of these and many more.
Mother says (that) we may play
In this simple, pretty way.
Count the jewels, roll the ball,
Have simplicity with all.

Unknown origin.

I have a little drum that Mother gave to me,
The prettiest little drum that ever you did see,
I'll drum night and day, I'll drum night and day,
To call volunteers to fight sin away.

Shirley.

Mother's love
Gold in the hand.
Mother's love
Gold in the hand.

Nov. 30, 1838. n.p.

A HANDFUL OF GOSPEL LOVE

Here's love by the handful
Here's love by the ball
Here's love for the Elders
Here's love for you all
This love it flows freely
From this little store
To all Mother's children
The wilderness ore.

Harvard, 1849.

[80] The song may have been sung by one person or a group, the singer or singers either standing, kneeling or moving about in a regular or irregular "dance." The reception of an individual or communal gift was usually attended by appropriate gestures, the reaching out of hands, bowing in thankfulness, etc. The "drinking" songs in which spiritual wine was received could have been placed in this classification.

THE GIFT TO BE SIMPLE

O the simple gifts of God,
They're flowing like an Ocean,
And I will strive with all my might
To gather in my portion.
I love I love the gifts of God,
I love to be partaker
And I will labor day & night
To be an honest Shaker.

*From Polly Champlain, of North
Union, to Luther C., n.d.*

WARRANTED LOVE

O here is a ball of my sweet love
Which I have rolled for you
O do receive each gospel friend
I'll warrant it sound and true
Sound and true, sound and true,
O do receive each gospel friend,
I'll warrant it sound and true.

Second family, New Lebanon. c. 1849.

The least of Mothers little love
Is good enough for me
Its more than I am worthy of
To send it unto me
Its very good its very sweet
I want nothing better
I'll not exchange it
For anything greater.

New Gloucester "Book of spiritual songs," n.d.

I have a little nog(g)in full of love sweet love
Mother sent me here with it to feed her simple doves
It is sweet it is sweet it is very sweet
Chick chick chick pretty chick come and eat.

New Gloucester hymnal, n.d.

MOTHER ANN'S PLUM CAKE

I have a plum cake,
A pretty little plum cake,
Will you eat a piece of it
Says blessed Mother.
Tis my love and blessing
For my dear children
O how I love you
I will be with you.

*From Elder Ebenezer (Bishop). New
Lebanon, Oct. 6, 1843.*

BALLS OF SIMPLICITY

My brethren and Sisters
I've got some little balls of Simplicity.
My blessed Father James did give them unto me,
O will you have some, they will make you free.

Henry B. Oct. 10, 1843. Place unknown.

BASKET OF TREASURES

Here's some pretty little baskets fill'd with love,
And many precious treasures says Mother's little dove.
Here are jewels and diamonds and many pretty rings,
I have borne them to you on my silver wings.
So good brethren and sisters I'm not bound,
If you will receive them I will throw them round.

New Gloucester, 1847.

SILVER CUP

Holy Mother give to me
A pretty little cup for thee
Fill'd with wine purest wine
Take the cup and drink it up.
O ho O ho I love Mother's wine
O ho O ho I'll drink every time.

*"Shouting song" from the Church family
(New Lebanon?) 1851.*

[67]

Fig. 9.—The text of the song is as follows:

> Our ministry's come who are faithful and true
> To help us and guide us on our journey thro
> Our kind loving friends who are now in our view
> To us are a treasure they're faithful and true
> And we'll make them welcome with uplifted hands
> From every subject in Zion's pure band.

Fig. 10.—Youngs' music manual, which he probably printed himself on a small hand-press, was widely used in singing meetings and in the Shaker schools at the time when interest in song was at its height. It was reprinted in 1846.

Figs. 11 and 11a.—In the actual writing of music, rests were seldom used. Youngs included several noted and worded songs in his manual as practice examples.

Fig. 12.—The tedious task of setting the letter-notes for the first Canterbury hymnal was performed by Elder Henry C. Blinn of that community. In the latter half of the nineteenth century this New Hampshire society was the publishing center of the Shaker order.

A Welcome Song.
99

FIG. 9

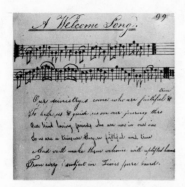

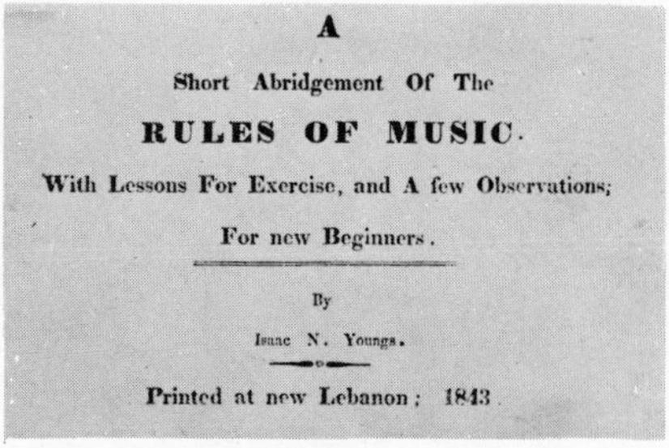

A

Short Abridgement Of The

RULES OF MUSIC.

With Lessons For Exercise, and A few Observations;

For new Beginners.

By

Isaac N. Youngs.

Printed at new Lebanon; 1843.

FIG. 10

37
A marching tune.
A square order shuffle

FIG. 11

11
VIEW OF THE LENGTH OF NOTES AND RESTS.
Names of gradation
Semibreves
Minims
Crotchets
Quavers
Semiquavers
Demisemiquavers
Notes.
Rests.
NOTE. The semibreve and minim rests are made alike, but one is placed below the line and the other above. The crotchet rest has its hook turn to the right, and the others turn to the left.
A semibreve is equal to two minims, or four crotchets, or eight quavers, or sixteen semiquavers, or thirty-two demisemiquavers.

FIG. 11a

HEAVENLY DISPLAY.
The waves of the ocean imitate the rolls of the heavenly
music that rolls in heaven. O le ul lum ul la, O le ul lum
ul la, O glory to God for this heavenly display.
2 The wheels of a time-piece imitate the flows of the heavenly love love that flows in heaven.
Chorus.
3 The wings of an eagle imitate the seraphim that soar in the heavens of heavenly love.
Chorus.
Given by inspiration, 1838.
New Lebanon, N. Y.

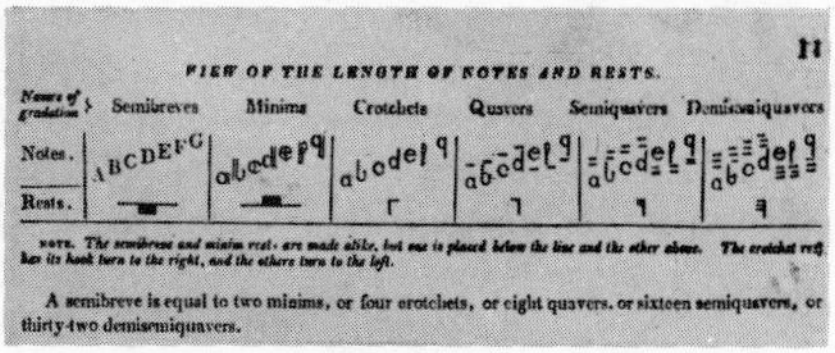

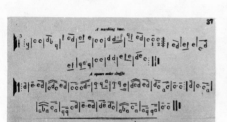

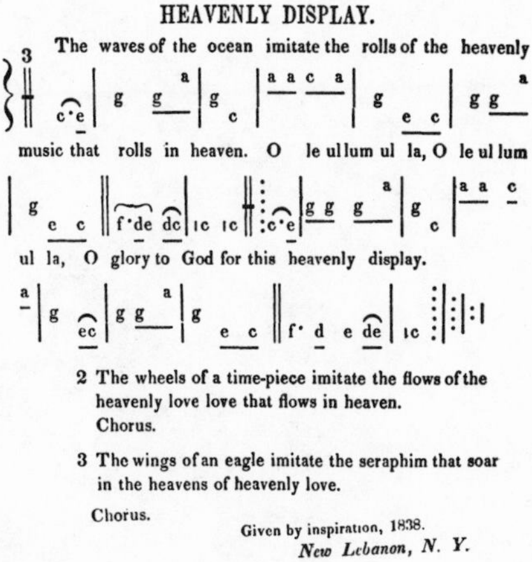

FIG. 12

So behold little ones, behold what I've got for you
1 2 3 4 5 6 7 8 9 & 10 thousand balls
Of your blessed Mother's love
O receive my little lambs, receive it from my hand.

> "*From the Shepherdess. Jan[y] 28th to
> Phebey Mosely.*"

THE NIGHTENGAL

Coo, coo, coo, coo
Chila cotha coo
I'll bring you Mother's love
I will bring you Mother's blessing,
It is a pretty treasure
A treasure worth possessing.

> *S. E. to J. W. (n.p., n.d.)*

BRIGHT DIAMOND

For my little Diamond bright
And my little golden seal
For my pretty pearl of Mother's love
How thankful I do feel
O fe ni fi ne fi feen
Fine fene fa
O ca ra an or az treen
Ar ge ne va.

> *Learned of Polly Billings & given to Jane
> Blanchard by E. Sister Olive. (New
> Lebanon) Dec.[m] 30-1838.*

5. "Indian" Songs.[81]

THE END OF MOURNING

De shiny Mother say to her children weep no more mourn
    no more for de vile hypocrit
Dis no purify you
Dis no strengthen you dis no comfort you one bit.

> *New Lebanon hymnal, n.d.*

[81] In these songs "the shiny (shiney) Mudder" refers to Mother Ann. The "shinys" are the white people ("whities").

THE SHOULDER BLANKETS

Me brought some pretty blankets
To keep the shiny's warm
Me place it on your shoulders
To shield you from the storm
The shiny Mother send them
She say you love such Things
The warp be her rich blessing
Her love be de filling.

Probably New Lebanon Second
family, about 1845.

MISTAKEN THOUGHT

Me can't see why the shiney's look is sober
Me thought the bad times was most over
Me wish you'd were (wear) de happy smile
For me take comfort *all* de while.

Unknown origin and date.

SQUAW SONG [82]

O here is love you com,
Que quaw quaw qui qum,
Here is love que cum
Qui quaw ka treen
Ka ke ke ka ki ke
Haw haw haw haw haw
Haw haw haw.

Away up in the heavens
A much big river I see,
It is flowing, it is flowing,
Flowing down on you and me.

Unknown origin.

[82] Sung to . . . in the Dary room, Sabbath evening by a little Squaw. June 23, 1839. (New Lebanon?)

Now see how spry me dance
How nimble me can labor
When me soul is fill'd wid lub
And Modder's holy power
Me will bow and me will turn
and dat will mux old nature
Den me hab de holy lub
and dat be much de better.

Church family, Shirley. October, 1845.

Me love come meety learn to tand,
Like whities trait & fold de hand,
Me tink dat dey look so pretty
Dat me like dem want be goody.
Me like learn toot toot on de trump
Me seen dem try how high dey jump;
Now me want learny singy too,
Me like learn dant as shiney do.

Church family, Shirley. 1845.

Now me've come down
From great big and up high,
Now me feel little,
Little and low.

Humility song. n.p., n.d.

O come Mother's little angel,
Gather near, me want to feel,
Me want to feel more life & zeal.
O me an wa wah, me an wa wah.

*Brought by a squaw from shiny Mudder for Joanna
K. October 16, 1842. New Lebanon, Second Order.*

Me bless the cross it brings me low,
It fits me for the Shiny Word.
Altho to lift it heavy be
What be beneath it comfort me.

Given at Holy Ground (Canterbury) June 17, 1847.

[71]

Ah pe-an t-as ke t-an te loo
O ne vas ke than sa-na was-ke
   lon ah ve shan too
Te wan-se ar ke ta-ne voo te
   lan se o-ne voo
Te on-e-wan tase va ne woo te wan-se o-ne van
Me-le wan se oo ar ke-le van te
   shom-ber on vas sa la too lar var sa
   re voo an don der on v-tar loo-cum an la voo
O be me-sum ton ton ton tol a wac—er tol-a wac-er
   ton ton te s-er pane love ten poo

By "Jack." Holy Ground. Oct. 6th 1847.

Wake up e wake up
And dant on e toe,
Wake up e wake up
And let de debil go.
O take limber teps,
And make fly
All dat belong to great big I.

Shirley Church, n.d.

A LITTLE PAPPOOSE SONG

Te ho te haw te hotti-ty hoot
Me be Mother's goody Pappoose
Me ting, me dant, te I didy um
Cause me to whity's here can come
Hi-de di-de ti diddle O
Round e round and round me go
Me leap me jump e up & down
On good whity shiny ground.

Shirley Church, n.d.

Me Indian come
Me come me stay
Me tanke de white man
He show me de way

[72]

He tell me to dig up
And fess all me sin
Dat make me look pretty
All whity and clean
Much pretty me feel
Much pretty me look
Me raise a de Indian
War a who whoop
Me catch wicket spirit
Me make him to yell
Me trike him me kick him
Me trow him to hell.

Unknown origin.

Now me happy feel
Now me limber
Now me tal-la-see
Noting hinder
Way moy wac a moy
Wa moy wip wip
Way moy wac-a-moy
Wip wip wip wip.

Unknown origin.

Me have some love from Mother Ann
Me love it love it dearly
She called me her little son
And made me feel cheerly.

Unknown origin.

Me rise me rise in mighty power
And show and show me Indian grit
Me trample down de soft de flat
And every ting dat be like dat.

Canterbury, n.d.

Me hab brat you lub & wampum
Me hab brat you cake & wine
Me hab brat you many presents
Dat will make de whity shine

Do receive de pretty presents
Just de best dat we can bring
Modder's pretty shiny children
O ho(w) dood to take us in.

Harvard, n.d.

AN INDIAN TUNE

Quo we lorezum qwini
    qui qwini qwe qwini qwe
Hock a nick a hick nick
    qwini qwi qwo cum.
Hack a ling shack a ling
    hick a chick a loreum,
Lal a ve lal a que
    qwi ac a qwo cum.

Often "used" at Hancock.

INDIAN MARCH

Now me feel so happy and free
Me can unite in de jubilee
Me can arise and blow me horn
Me can rejoice at night and morn
Me can be happy while moving around
Stepping on de solemn sound
Me can unite in de solemn dance
Praising God as me advance.

Unknown origin.

Me want to feel de whity's love
Me love it in the dance to move
No more will Indian have to rove
Me got into de bright land.
No squaw dat ever did me see
To shine like Mudder Anna Lee
She tell if Indian will be free
She'll love him well de white man.

Church family, Enfield, N. H.

THE GREEN PIDGEON

Me want me want whity's pretty treasure
Me want me want love love love love
Chocane chocane choctaw choctaw.

Unknown origin.

ARKUMSHAW'S FAREWELL

Me tanke de white man who for me did fess
Me tank de good Elder whom he did address
Me feel poor and needy me want me soul save
And now lest me weary de white man me leave.

Unknown origin.

Do um feel what um be like a teter back and forth
Like de leavs on de tree when de wind does blow um much
Such must be my pretty children at de Elders precious word
They must move um in obedience or me cannot send um love.

From a Maine hymnal, n.d.

Me hold up de one foot and dance on de udder
And all de time me sing de praise to de blessed Mudder
Me hop up de once and de twice and de tree times
And all de time me sing de praise to de blessed Mudder.

Sabbathday Lake, n.d.

O look e ye and see de many pretty tings
Dese be de shine(y) jewels and many gold rings
Me shake them all ore you me chinker chinker chink
And while you have de freedom O hark and hear them tink.

Sabbathday Lake, 1848.

6. *"Negro" Songs.*

E ne me ne mo del e
Sanc to luro lu ral lee
Lu ral lan do me ne see
Pa ri an dor hoo sa me.

Enfield, N. H. May 2, 1838.
"Negro" song in unknown tongue.

[75]

Come Mother's love and fill my soul,
Come Mother's love and fill my soul,
Mother's love is freedom, Mother's love is good,
Come Mother's love and fill my soul.

> *"Given on the Holy Mount by a colored spirit named Jack through Abm Perkins August 30, 1847." Enfield, N. H.*

What makes you look so sober, what makes you feel so sad,
Is it because you're weary or are you almost mad,
If not then cast off sadness and wear the pleasant smile,
And with we African spirits be simple as a child.
For lo my Mother told me to come and carress you,
Each brother and each sister with love both sweet & new,
And here it is I'll toss it round, give you all a portion,
And everyone that catches some twill set them all in motion.

> *Sabbathday Lake hymnal, n.d.*

7. Songs in Unknown Tongues.[83]

VIVE VUM

Vive vo vive vum, vive vum vum vo,
Vive vo vive vum, vive vum vum vo,
Vive vo vive vum, vive vum vum vo,
Vive vo vive vum, vive vum vum vo.

> *Given at the North family, New Lebanon. From Mother Ann to Sister Aseneth. June 26th 1843.*

A DREAM

(A song in "strange" tongues, with "interpretation.")

O sa ri anti va me	O Saviour wilt thou hear me
O sa ri anti va me	O Saviour wilt thou hear me
I co lon se ve re	I am poor and kneedy
I con e lo se va ne	I'll come and bow before thee
I con e lo se va ne	I'll come and bow before thee
Se ran te lo me.	Thy cross I'll take upon me.

> *By E. D.-East family, New Lebanon, Dec. 1845.*

[83] For other examples of unknown tongues, see songs 35-38, also vision songs below.

8. Vision Songs

Lowly is the soul that crieth to God,
low, low, low, low, low, low.
Love, love is pretty love flowing from our Mother.
Love, love is pretty love flowing from the fountain
low, low, low.

*Sally Vanvyke. Hill Family (New
Lebanon) vision tune. Jan. 1838.*

TRUMP OF FREEDOM

Blow ye the trump of freedom
and join the tripple band.
For God will surely lead you
on to the promis' land.

*"From Elder Sr. Olive to Isaac N. Youngs. Given
while working at the carding Machine by one of the
inspired sisters. Wens. eve. Sep 29th 1840."*

Shake shake shake in the valley low.
Down down low low
down down low low
down down low low
down down low low.

Mary Wicks. New Lebanon, March 25-1838.

Holy Angels are a bowing unto God
They're teaching us our souls must bow
They're teaching us our souls must bow
to ev'ry gift of God.
O I will bow, low, low, low
down low, low, low
I'll bow my soul.

*Eleanor Potter. New Lebanon, March 28, 1838.
("Tunes given to E. P. in various ways. Some
nights other's day times.")*

[77]

Cry unto God for repentance true
Wash wash wash and be clean.

> *"Given in meeting Sat-ev. Novem....2nd 1839 by
> Chiles Hamlin. Father Joseph was present he
> said he brought Chiles with him to sing this song.
> he said it was one they sung in heaven when they
> were* called to repent." *The song was used in a
> purification ritual.*

WASH & BE CLEAN

Come, Come, Come to the fountain
    all ye that are poor and needy;
    and strip off your garment that's old
    and wash and be clean pure and holy.
Then you shall be Mother's Children.
O what an Ocean of pure love
I'll strip off my garment that's old
I'll wash and be clean pure and holy
Then Mother will love me
    she'll own me and bless me
    and give me a robe that is pure.

> *Eliza Sharpe's gift or vision song. New Lebanon?
> April, 1838.*

9. *Vision Songs (wholly or partly in unknown tongues)*

Hoo haw hum necatry O necatry O
Hoo haw hum necatry O cum
Ne holium ne-holium ne-catry O ne-catry O
Ne holium ne-holium ne hoo haw hum.

> *Hannah Ann Agnew. New Lebanon 1838.*

O werekin werekin catry catry
Werekin werekin catry co
O werekin werekin catry catry
Werekin werekin catry coo.

> *Hannah Ann Agnew. New Lebanon 1838.*

A MARCH

One way ne wick um wum ne
Wum ne wick um wum
O wick um wum
O wick um wum
One way ne wick um wum.

Sarah VanVyke. 1843. Oct.

Via lo via le via le er lan do
Via lo via le via lo ra lorum
Father is the lead come let us all be free
That we may have a portion
Of Mothers love and blessing.

*"George Washingtons, one of the former Presidents
of the United States." Given in vision at Canterbury, 1838.*

10. Songs of Humility.[84]

DISMISSION OF GREAT I

Go off great I, and come not nigh
But quit my habitation
And come no more within my door
Corrupting my sensation
Depart I say flee far away
Your ways no more I'll practice
For all who try to be great I
Are vicious, proud and fractious.

I now disclaim that great big name
And all my title to it
That great big I, I'll mortify
No pity will I show it
It may elope but need not hope
To share in my salvation
Tho' near of kin, a nat'ral twin
By Adam's old relation.

Early Shaker anthem.

[84] Songs of humility—"low songs"—may be anthems, dance songs, ritualistic or gestural songs, or vision songs.

Come, holy angels, quickly come,
And bring your purifying fire;
Consume our lusts in every home,
And root out every foul desire.

Watervliet, previous to 1838.[85]

WALK SOFTLY

When we assemble here to worship God,
To sing his praises & to hear his word
We will walk softly.

With purity of heart; and with clean hands,
Our souls are free, we're free from Satan's bands
We will walk softly.

While we are passing thro' the sacred door,
Into the fold where Christ has gone before,
We will walk softly.

We'll worship and bown down we will rejoice
And when we hear the shepherds gentle voice
We will walk softly.

Early Shaker anthem.

---

[85] This might be called a "prayer song." The whole assembly, in ranks, fell on their knees, and "elevating their hands and arms, and making signs of beckoning or invitation," sang the song over and over again. At the conclusion of every verse they bowed their heads to the ground and at the end remained on their knees for some time, looking steadfastly at the floor—"buried in the most profound silence." (Buckingham, pp. 59-60.) Compare with the Methodist hymn:

Come, Holy Spirit, heavenly dove,
With all thy quick'ning powers,
Kindle a flame of sacred love
In these cold hearts of ours.

(*Attributed to Brainerd, "Methodist Hymns,"
1842, p. 125.*)

MOTHER'S CHILD

Just as Mother says
I want to do
O I feel very humble and low
If she wants me to shake
Turn or reel
Just as Mother says I do feel.

Unknown origin.

I will bow and be simple
I will bow and be free
I will bow and be humble
Yea bow like the willow-tree
I will bow this is the token
I will wear the easy yoke
I will bow and be broken
Yea I'll fall upon the rock.

North family. New Lebanon?

Whoever wants to be the highest
Must first come down to be the lowest;
And then ascend to be the highest
By keeping down, to be the lowest.

From Enfield, N. H., n.d.

Come down Shaker-like
Come down holy
Come down Shaker-like
Let's all go to glory.

Early Pleasant Hill (Ky.) song.

MOTHER'S LITTLE EYE

Great eye little eye great eye can see,
Little eye is pretty eye little I will be,
Little eye simple eye little eye is free,
Little eye is pretty eye little I will be.

Unknown origin.

[81]

THE GIFT TO BE SIMPLE

Down Down I mean to go
And think but little of it.
Mother loves the meek and low
And why am I above it.[86]

Second family, New Lebanon. c. 1847.

COMING DOWN A LITTLE

O Brethren & Sisters we'll come down,
Come down a little lower;
Keep pulling down, keep pulling down,
Come down a little lower.

The gifts of God we there shall find,
They're for the meek and lowly;
By coming down, yea coming down,
Coming a little lower.

Second family, New Lebanon. c. 1849.

[86] From a collection of sacred songs transcribed by Clarissa Jacobs. Curious titles in Sister Clarissa's book are Noggin of Love, Very Soft & occasionally Flat, Limber Zeal, Your Room is Better than your Company, Chaff Consuming furnace, Wonderful Pretty Form, Its Plenty Good Enough, A good Resolution if put in Practice. Sharp Sword begins, "Whittle, whittle, whittle;" Humble Position, "Lay low lay low lowly lie."

II.

TUNES AND MUSIC

On the authority of Brother Isaac N. Youngs, the Shaker historian, we learn that for several years after the meeting-house was built at New Lebanon (1785) the songs and tunes of the order were often "such as originated in the world." Already we have noted how the Believers, like the primitive Methodists and Baptists before them, copied or adapted religious and secular melodies, some of them "solemn" in mood, others with the lively tempo suited to the enthusiasm and spirited exercises of Shaker worship. A few tunes, we have seen, may be identified.by internal evidence. Another source of information exists, the reports of visitors who attended the public worship of the order during the years of its development and vitality. These accounts throw additional light on the nature of early tunes and the ways in which they were sung.

The English dance-song, "Nancy Dawson,"[1] for instance, was a favorite number when President Timothy Dwight of Yale visited the New Lebanon colony in 1798. James Silk Buckingham heard the same melody at Niskeyuna thirty years later; and in 1840 Lt. Col. Maxwell encountered it again at the Enfield (Conn.) community. Buckingham wrote that it was a common song, especially among sailors, in his English boyhood, though he had not heard it for over thirty years. The Shaker words, as recorded by this traveler, were:

> Press on, press on, ye chosen band,
> The angels go before ye;
> We're marching through Emanuel's land,
> Where saints shall sing in glory.

[1] The repute of Nancy Dawson (c. 1730-1767) rested chiefly on a horn-pipe dance which she performed in Gay's "Beggar's Opera," staged at Covent Garden, London, in 1759. The tune was afterwards set to words with the title, "The Ballad of Nancy Dawson" or "Nancy Dawson's song." A correspondent in "Notes and Queries" wrote that the tune was like that of the children's play-song, "Here we go round the mulberry bush;" another remembered it as a stirring march which became a popular military piece.

As the worshippers "scampered around the room in a quick gallopade," the song wrought them "to such a high pitch of fervour, that they were evidently on the point of some violent outbreak or paroxysm."[2]

On a visit to New Lebanon in 1790, William Loughton Smith, member of congress and friend of Washington, heard the Shaker women "howling sundry strange tunes," one of which was called "The Black Joke."[3] From Smith's and Dwight's journals, as well as from the reports of Rathbun, Benjamin West and Amos Taylor, the impression is unmistakable that the characteristic tunes of Ann Lee's day and the years immediately following her death, were extremely animated and weirdly discordant. With the rise of Joseph Meacham to power, however, and the transference of energy to the tasks of communal organization, the meetings grew more orderly and restrained. In the decade of Father Joseph's ministry, from 1786 to 1796, increased emphasis was placed on hymns expressive of mortification and deep humility, the so-called "solemn songs," which, when "properly" sung, proceeded from "deep in the throat or breast."

"Merry tunes" regained favor in the course of Lucy Wright's ministry (1796-1821). "Yankee Doodle" and "Over the river to Charley," for example, had for some time been popular at the Enfield (N. H.) society when Mary Dyer wrote her "Portraiture of Shakerism" in 1822. At a "union meeting" which she attended there were pipes to smoke, melons and apples and nuts to eat, and cider to drink. Sitting in two rows facing each other, the brethren and sisters sang such "merry love songs" as

> I love the brethren, the brethren love me,
> O! how happy, how happy I be.
> I love the sisters, the sisters love me,
> O! how the happy, how happy I be.
> How pretty they look, how clever they feel,
> And this we will sing when we love a good deal.[4]

[2] Buckingham, J. S. America, Historical, Statistic, and Descriptive. Vol. II, p. 61. New York, 1841.

[3] Journal of William Loughton Smith, 1790-1791. (In Proceedings of the Massachusetts Historical Society, October, 1917-June, 1918. Vol. LI. Boston, 1918.) "Black Joke" was an English morris-dance. Several tunes supposed to have been sung by Mother Ann, Father William, Father James and others at Harvard, Hancock, New Lebanon, etc. in the period 1780-1784 were later recorded. (MS. hymnals in author's collection. Also Sears, Clara Endicott: Gleanings from Old Shaker Journals, pp. 70, 109, 117, 155, 163, 183. Boston, 1916.)

[4] Dyer, Mary. A Portraiture of Shakerism, pp. 279-280. Concord, 1822. The tune is not given.

Fig. 13.—The Canterbury leaflet-songs, written to simple tunes, marked the first step in the adoption of standard, round-note notation. "More Love" belongs to the period of the early 1870's.

Fig. 14.—The square-order dance.

The tempo of the circular dance song, "Perpetual Blessings," heard by Buckingham at Watervliet in 1838, was like "the allegro of a sonata, or the vivace of a canzonet." The tune was "Scots wha' ha'e wi' Wallace bled," sung rapidly "such as is sometimes done when it is converted into a quick march by a military band." The song itself—

> Perpetual blessings do demand,
> Perpetual praise on every hand;
> Then leap for joy, with dance and song,
> To praise the Lord forever—

was something between a march and a dance, repeated over and over for about five minutes. The bodies of the worshippers, two abreast, inclined forward like persons running; "perfect time" was kept with the feet and the hands, which "beat the air;" some literally leaped, so high that when they struck the floor it jarred the meeting-room.

The gaiety of such songs and dances often astonished the spectators, who came expecting the solemnity of an orthodox religious service. After attending a meeting at Enfield in 1840, Maxwell wrote:

If the Shakers' doctrine be the true one, our system of kneeling and praying ought immediately to give place to singing merry songs and dancing Scotch reels. . . . I never beheld the double-shuffle, the cut the buckle, and the Highland fling in greater perfection.![5]

The first Enfield hymn was like "a good heart-stirring old English hunting-song." "Chevy Chase" was the next tune. Then came the old favorite "Nancy Dawson," followed by such "elegant and pious" tunes as "The D—l among the Tailors" and "Moll in the Wad." At a meeting at Watervliet about the same period (1839), the Scotch phrenologist George Combe similarly observed that "their tunes were merry measures, with strongly marked time, such as are played in farces and pantomimes.[6]

[5] Maxwell, Lieut.-Col. A. M., K. H. A Run through the United States, during the autumn of 1840. In two volumes. Vol. I, pp. 90-91. London: 1841.

[6] (Joel Munsell, ed.) Collections on the History of Albany, Vol. II, p. 347. Albany, 1867. "While singing (Combe wrote) they knelt occasionally . . . By-and-by some of them began to bend their bodies forwards, to shake from side to side, and to whirl round. A favorite motion was to let the trunk of the

Songs and tunes became even more spirited as "Mother Ann's Work" got under way. In a procession to the holy fountain at Wisdom's Valley (Watervliet) in 1843, Macdonald saw the participants playing on spiritual "golden instruments:"

Each one (he wrote) made a sound with the mouth, to please him or herself, and at the same time, went through the motions of playing some particular instrument, such as the Clarionet, French Horn, Trombone, Bass Drum, etc. and such a noise was made that I felt as if I had got amongst a parcel of Lunatics. It appeared to me much more of a Burlesque Overture, than I had heard performed by Christys Minstrels on the Cow Bells.[7]

Harmonious singing was a gradual development. As we have observed, instruction in musical notation was fragmentary until the end of the first quarter of the nineteenth century. The early Shakers were as indifferent to melody as to art in any other form. For a hundred years after Ann Lee landed in America instrumental music was also banned—being considered "superfluous," "formal," "worldly," "diverting" and "inferior to vocal music." Rationalizing an attitude which may well have been inherited from the Quakers, the Believers argued that the use of instruments would breed pride in the performers, that it tended to disunion, that it covered "imperfections which should be revealed."[8] Without even a dulcimer or harp to assist the melody, no wonder that praise resounded in a "tumultuous discord."

From the time, however, that Seth Wells first proposed that music be taught in the schools and family gatherings, the "singing meeting" slowly grew in importance. An occasional allusion indicates its character. Probably the "class" consisted of the best singers, male and female, in the family—those who on the Sabbath were to lead the communal songs and dances in public worship. The

---

body drop downwards, with a sudden jerk, to one side, care being taken always to recover the perpendicular before the equilibrium was lost. The head and trunk were drawn up by another jerk. In all their shakings and contortions they never lost the step in their dance, nor ran against each other...."

[7] Macdonald MS., op. cit.

[8] Instrumental music was not sanctioned until 1870, when the standard notation replaced the letter-notes of Shaker tradition. A melodium or small cabinet organ was purchased at Canterbury in that year, and two years later a convert brought in a piano. By 1874 instruction in music, assisted by a melodium or harmonium, was spread by Canterbury teachers to New Lebanon, Watervliet and as far west as South Union, Ky. A quartet composed of sisters was organized at Canterbury in the late 1880's.

instructor—an individual specially appointed "to study and obtain a knowledge of the rules in the best way he could"—would set the pitch, either by ear or a tuning-fork, and keep time with his hand or foot, the class following his lead as he lined out the tune. There is evidence that the pitch was sometimes set and guided by a "toneometer;"[9] and when instruction had reached a certain stage, time was also measured by the swing of a bullet attached to a string.[10] At a later period, when the increased production of songs necessitated more frequent practice sessions, the union meetings were sometimes devoted to singing.

The musical theory and practice of the early Shakers were essentially the same as that which we find in use generally and in those same times in rural singing circles. The first known tune books of the sect had the same round-note manner of tune writing[11] and the same tune forms used in non-Shaker circles. Since the general "science" of popular music, as delineated in scores of old singing-school manuals of song and even in many religious tune books of the times, is fairly well known, it is not necessary to discuss the points in which the Shaker tradition is in agreement with it. The brief survey which follows, contributed by Dr. George Pullen Jackson of Vanderbilt University, is chiefly concerned with those phases and later peculiarities of Shaker musical theory which represent a departure from the normal and standard.

The initial steps towards an unworldly concept of musical writing were taken sometime between 1820 and 1825, the period in which the first Shaker singing classes were organized. Someone at the Harvard community, claiming to have been inspired by Mother Ann, argued that both the writing and the reading of music would be simplified if letters were used in place of round notes.[12] For several years the Harvard and Shirley societies experimented with

[9] The toneometer, credited as a Shaker invention, was a kind of monochord or tone-measurer, a one-stringed instrument so marked that it could give any pitch desired.

[10] In his manual on the Rules of Music, printed in 1843, Isaac Youngs recommended, for beginners, a "speediometer (an instrument already well known)—to vibrate or swing once in a second." "A bullet," he suggested, "attached to a smooth string, 39½ inches long, from the point of suspension, to the center of the ball, will very nearly vibrate seconds."

[11] A single song in the four-shape notation (Fig. 9) remains unexplained. Did it represent a ray of influence from the nearby Albany, New York, neighborhood of the eighteenth century? The Shaker song stands alone as a sign of New England acceptance of the notational style which had already spread into all parts south and west where, incidentally, it still lives and thrives. Cf. Jackson, *White Spirituals in the Southern Uplands,* especially p. 11 ff.

[12] The idea of letter notation may have come from the Reverend John Tufts, a minister of Newburyport, Mass., in whose book—"A very plain and easy introduction to the whole Art of Singing

the system, trying out various methods to indicate the length of the notes: capitalization, italics, sloping letters backwards, and so on.[13] Finally, at New Lebanon, a method was adopted and standardized in which *small* letters were used, with brevitures attached to indicate their length, the only letter to be capitalized being the whole note or semibreve. Musical values, therefore, were as follows:

$$\bigcirc = A \qquad\qquad \text{♩} = a \qquad\qquad \text{♪} = \bar{\bar{a}}$$

$$\text{♩} = a\text{|} \qquad\qquad \text{♪} = \bar{a} \qquad\qquad \text{♬} = \bar{\bar{\bar{a}}}$$

The new method apparently made its way very slowly, for "letteral" notation did not appear in the manuscript tune books of the sect until 1837 and it was not until the next decade that Youngs and Haskell published their manuals of instruction on the Shaker system.[14]

"Perhaps the most striking point of variance with outside tradition found in these book sources (comments Dr. Jackson) is the notation the compilers used. In place of the orthodox symbols for notes, they used the letters *a b c d e f g* and in this order ascending. These letters, while they are the same as those used generally, then as now, did not stand for *fixed pitch* entities but rather for *comparative melodic* entities. No matter on what *absolute* pitch level the tune was keyed, *c* was its basic note if it was a major tune and *d* was basic if minor. The series of letters thus represented the Shaker equivalent to the moveable faw-sol-law system of the early English and of the rural *Sacred Harp* singers in the southern uplands today and to the moveable do-re-mi system imported into America somewhat over a century ago.[15] The Shaker letteral notes were called

Psalm tunes," first published in 1712—letters were used instead of notes and time marked by one or more dots to the right of the letter. This early eastern-Massachusetts instruction book, which went into several editions, might well have been known to members of the Harvard community. (See Earle, Alice Morse: The Sabbath in Puritan New England, p. 207. New York, 1891. Also Howard, John Tasker: Our American Music, p. 14. New York, 1930-1931.)

[13] In the original Harvard system, the first seven letters of the alphabet replaced the notes of standard usage. Eighth notes were written in italics, quarter notes in Roman and half notes as plain capitals with a single upright line placed after them.

[14] Youngs, Isaac N. A Short Abridgement of the Rules of Music. With Lessons for Exercise, and a few Observations; for New Beginners. New Lebanon, 1843. (Reprinted in 1846.) See Fig. 10. Haskell, Russel. A Musical Expositor: or, a treatise on the rules and elements of music; adapted to the most approved method of musical writing. New York, 1847.

[15] Cf. Jackson, G. P., White Spirituals, especially pages 4 and 319.

either by their alphabetical names or by the names al, be, co, do, en, faw, goo. Neither Youngs nor Haskell looked upon these note-names as anything more than occasionally necessary evils. Youngs granted that they might be used by those 'who feel so disposed.' Haskell insisted that 'the notes should not be frequently sounded on *any* particular set of syllables or names: but sometimes the names of the letters may be used, and once in a while all (notes) may be sung on the syllable *va* or *ve;* but oftener on the syllables *lo-do-le.*'[16]

STAFFLESS TUNES

"Both Youngs and Haskell tell of 'the five lines on which music is written;' but Youngs doesn't *use* it at all, and Haskell uses it only occasionally. The manuscript tune books show the same condition,—a sparing use of the staff; some occurrence of a single line with the letter-notes placed on it or above or below at distances which indicate adequately their relative pitch; and much complete discarding of all lines, leaving the letters and their placing as the only indications of relation and pitch. This doing away with the staff may have been suggested to the Shaker tune writers by a similar innovation attempted in the early years of that century by the prominent singing master and song-book compiler, Andrew Law of Connecticut; even though Law used shape-notes, not letters.[17] But it is more probable, especially in view of what looks like a *gradual* desuetude of the staff, that the tune writers and singers slowly realized that they could get along without it, and did.

RYHTHMIC FREEDOM

"The barring of the Shaker tunes is indicated, as in our music, by vertical lines. Unique symbols, however, are used at the beginning and on occasion within the tunes to indicate tempo and the type of measure or time formula, even though those tempi and types of measure are the same as ours. After examining the

[16] The expense of a printing-type adapted to the "letteral" system and the difficulty of setting such type possibly account in part for the fact that no printed hymn books, with music included, appeared in the society until 1852. Some type, it is true, was cut for Youngs' manual, probably by himself, but a great deal more would have been necessary in the composition of an entire hymnal. In Haskell's "Musical Expositor" all the Shaker notes and other symbols were inserted, presumably by the author, by hand with pen and ink. A page from "The Sacred Repository," the only hymnal published with letter notes, is illustrated in Fig. 12.

[17] Cf. *White Spirituals*, pp. 11-13 and illustration opposite p. 22. Andrew Law (1748-1821) was the compiler of "Select Harmony" (1778) and "A Collection of Best Tunes and Anthems" (1779), both widely used in New England.

tunes in the manuscript Shaker books, however, one must come to the conclusion that measure types are far from having the binding or regularizing force that they exert in hymns generally. For we find often in one and the same tune a number of measure types, some of them represented by but a few measures or even only one.[18] And as the succeeding measures refuse to conform to regular patterns, so also do the tune forms as wholes. One may look long without finding a song constructed on one of the standard hymn-tune plans. And the extreme degree of this irregularity appears in those long, rambling concoctions to which the Shakers gave the name 'anthems.' Causes of this lack of what we call form may be sought (a) in the fact that the songs are the products of individuals, and (b) that such productions were not subjected to that *zersingen* process which comes from wide and general singing over long periods of time; (c) in the ritualistic functions of many of the songs and (d) in the unusual demands of the texts themselves to which the tunes had to yield.

FOLK-MANNER IN SINGING

"There is still another convention of standard hymn-tunes to which the Shakers refused to conform. I refer to the hoary custom of presenting the melody in what is nothing more than a skeletonic or schematic form, leaving the singers to fill out that form as their feeling and their *folk-manner of singing* dictated. (The country singers themselves now call it 'twisting' the tune, or 'turning the corners.') Three conditions occur to me as reasons why compilers of standard religious tune books avoided tune twisting: (1) they inherited a great body of the skeletonic tunes, (2) they faced difficulties in putting such notational complications into type, and (3) they knew that 'turning the corners' was inimical to the effectiveness of the harmonic part-singing which they fostered. The Shakers however—having inherited no recorded song tradition, holding their notational scheme in their own hands, and not being bothered by part-singing at all—wrote down their tunes, as far as they were able, just as they were sung,—in the folk-manner.

"I cannot define the country- or folk-manner; it is too intangible. It may suffice here to list some of its more obvious characteristics. They are (a) the upward slide to the beginning note of the tune; (b) bridging of intervals

---

[18] The changing rhythm and meter of many Shaker songs, expressed in a shifting of tune-signature, are illustrated by several tunes used in this book. Such changes, though unorthodox, permitted a fluency and freedom in musical writing.

(glissandi or anticipatory raising or lowering the vocal pitch in the direction of a following note; (c) the pitch sag between two successive notes which have the same pitch; (d) the Scotch snap, and (e) vocal quavers (sometimes called trills). The Shakers represented these, whenever they could, by their regular letter notes; but now and then they had recourse to symbols similar to our 'grace' notes. The following tune fragment from Haskell may throw a little light on the Shaker practice.

FIG. A

Come heav - en - ly love, and dwell with me for - ev - er.

a and e are gap-bridging notes or glissandi.
b and f are sags between two notes of the same pitch.
c and g are Scotch snaps.
d is an anticipatory rise on a comparatively wide interval.
h is the equivalent of a trill.

All these are characteristic of the folk-style in singing. Only one of them are designated by the tune writer as a grace note. (Haskell, p. 81. Original score in letter notation.)

HORIZONTAL HARMONY

" 'Harmony' is one of the topics discussed in the Shaker instruction books. Youngs disposes of it in one sentence of which I quote a part: —— 'as our society does not practice singing —— with several parts moving together, it will be unnecessary here to take much further notice of this branch of music.' So he takes *no* further notice of it. Haskell, too, refuses to discuss harmony, at least vertical harmony, and for the same reason. But when we examine his 26 pages of discussion under his heading 'Melody' we find he approaches his subject from what we would call the horizontal-harmonic point of view; for he discusses there the matter of the consonance or dissonance of successive tones. But his intrinsic contributions to the subject are restricted by its inherent difficulties, those which have remained unexplained or debatable to this day. Haskell's thoughts should receive attention in some more specialized study. They are out of place in this brief survey of Shaker music.

DORIAN NATURE OF SHAKER "MINOR"

"That the Shaker note *c* becomes the basis of all major diatonic tone sequences will seem natural enough. But the selection of *d* as the basic note for what they called 'minor' tunes is unique. For it will be seen that the diatonic sequence built upon that note (as when the white keys of the piano are sounded from *d* to *d*) gives neither the harmonic minor or orthodox musical usage nor the natural minor, but the scale of the *dorian mode*. In this we may see a radical departure from rural theory then current. The rural singing-school theory of constructing minor tunes held that they must begin on the third below the relative major tonic, or on *a* if we think of related major tonic as *c,* and use the tones represented by the white keys of the piano. This would result in a natural minor or an *aeolian modal* sequence. In brief, the singing-schools arbitrarily forced dorian tunes into the same mould with the aeolian tunes; and the Shakers, equally as arbitrarily, forced aeolian tunes into the dorian mould. In doing this both groups were wrong. There should have been room for two moulds, two varieties of 'minor,' the dorian and the aeolian, in their theories just as the two modes did appear in their actual singing practice. The Shaker scales, major and (dorian) minor, beginning respectively on their *c* and *d,* and the Shaker aeolian scale (with its sixth raised to meet Haskell's convictions as to *its* dorian nature) are given in Fig. B."

FIG. B

Musical alphabet in its simplest form, beginning first on *c,* and then on *d,* and having the place of each semitone marked ½.*

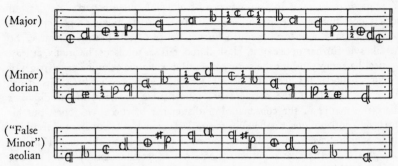

* The *c* and *d* scales are from Haskell, p. 45; the *a* "false minor" from Haskell, p. 50.

Haskell is not dogmatic in his modal reflections and judgments. To his mind (which I take to be a keen one) there are exceptions to all rules for scale construction. He sees, for example, cases where the "shrill air of melody" (the dorian character of tune) and the "soft air" (major or ionian characteristics) are mixed in one and the same tune, and gives (on p. 73) as an illustration the following "ancient solemn song:"

FIG. C

We should call this an essentially mixolydian tune.

The Shakers divided meter into three "modes"—even, triple and compound—and their submeasures:

Shaker mode	*Meter*	*Sign*
Even	4 / 4	
Submeasure of even	2 / 4	
Triple	3 / 4	
Compound	6 / 8	
Submeasure of compound	3 / 8	

[93]

The sign was placed at the beginning of the measure or measures to which it applied. The tempo of a song was set by means of a number from 1 to 4 placed above the "mode" sign, indicating the Shaker concept of Adagio, Largo, Allegro and Presto.

It was Youngs' aim to standardize the time of dance tunes, marches, "hymn songs" and anthems, and by so doing bring order and uniformity into the various parts of worship. With this in mind he prescribed the following "application of the modes and times:"[19]

Even Mode

First speed (or time) . . . . for slow funeral songs and other solemn songs.

Second speed . . . . for songs having alternately one longer note and two shorter ones, as a crotchet and two quavers.

Third speed . . . . for songs "a degree slower than the greater portion of common hymns;" also "for all even timed marches and quick dance tunes, which go in submeasure."

Fourth speed . . . . for most anthems and common even-timed hymns.

Submeasures of even mode . . . . . come in use "to accommodate to broken parts of full measures," the speed corresponding to "what precedes;" also for those songs which go in submeasure.

Triple Mode

All four speeds (called "adagio triple," "largo triple," etc.) . . . . "for such music as requires three equal timed beats to one principal accent;" also for broken parts of full measures.

[19] Youngs, Isaac N. A Short Abridgement of the Rules of Music, pp. 37-38.

Compound Mode

First speed . . . . for "slowest compound songs."

Second speed . . . . for parts of anthems when they change from even to compound mode.

Third speed . . . . also for use in such changes.

Fourth speed . . . . was the medium speed of the early square order shuffle. (As this fourth speed was not quick enough for certain "exercise songs," Youngs proposed a fifth and sixth speed—the latter as fast as the swing of a piece of weighted string an inch and a half long.)

First speed, compound submeasure . . . for common circular march.

Second speed, compound submeasure . . for square order shuffle.

Third speed, compound submeasure . . for round dance shuffle.

Fourth speed, compound submeasure . . for quick dance compound tunes.

The following chart indicates the various speeds:[20]

Mode	No. of seconds per measure	Beats per measure	Beats per minute	Length of string in inches
Even (1st speed, Adagio)	3	4	80	22
Even (2nd speed, Largo)	2⅝	4	91	17
Even (3rd speed, Allegro)	2¼	4	106	12½
Even (4th speed, Presto)	1⅞ to 1½	4	128 to 160	8¾ to 5½
Submeasures of even mode	half that of even mode	half that of even mode	same as even mode	same as even mode
Triple	three-quarters that of even mode	3	same as even mode	same as even mode
Compound (1st speed, Adagio)	2¼	4	106	12½
Compound (2nd speed, Largo)	1⅞	4	122	9½
Compound (3rd speed, Allegro)	1⅝	4	142	7
Compound (4th speed, Presto)	1⅜ to 1⅛	4	170 to 213	4¾ to 3⅛
Compound (5th speed)	1⅛	4	213	3⅛
Compound (6th Speed)	⅞ to ¾	4	250 to 300	2¼ to 1½
Sub measures of compound mode	half that of compound mode	half that of compound mode	same as compound mode	same as compound mode

Examination of a number of hymnals of the 1840's reveals that quick songs were usually written in 2/4, marches in 2/4 or 6/8, shuffling and round dance songs in 6/8, and extra songs in 2/4, 3/4, 4/4 or 6/8 time.

[20] Youngs, op. cit. "Table of Modes," pp. 30-31. Note that there are two sets of speed values, one for "even" and one for "compound mode."

1. MOTHER ANN'S SONG

A plaintive tune ascribed to Mother Ann. The date, 1782, in the Mary Hazzard MS. where it was found, makes it one of the earliest Shaker songs to be recorded. (See also Nos. 2-3.) The tune has a continental, old Bohemian (?) quality.

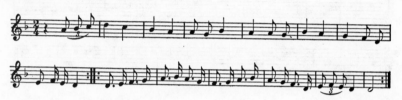

2. FATHER JAMES' SONG

From a hymnal transcribed by Mary Hazzard, of the New Lebanon Church family, in 1847. A note at the end of the score reads: "This song Father James sung when he was upon earth; Preserved in the Church at Hancock." The tune, therefore, dates back to the early 1780's. Since nearly all early Shaker songs are wordless, it is possible that the text of the present example was added at a later period. The time signature "4" ($\downarrow$=128-160) in the original manuscript is the Shaker presto. The song may be sung in the key of E flat; first note, B flat.

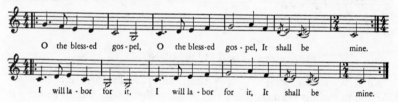

O the bless-ed gos-pel, O the bless-ed gos-pel, It shall be mine.

I will la-bor for it, I will la-bor for it, It shall be mine.

3. FATHER JAMES' SONG

This wordless song Father James was supposed to have sung at Harvard, Mass. as he was kneeling on the spot where he had just been scourged by an angry mob of townspeople. Date, 1783. The song was found in an old manuscript at Harvard, written in letter-notes, perhaps by someone who had been at the scene. Also in Hazzard MS. To be sung slowly and solemnly.

4. PRIMITIVE DANCE TUNE (1790)

Dated 1790 in the Hazzard (1847) hymnal from which it is taken. The evidence seems to indicate that this was a very fast, and of course a "wordless" tune.

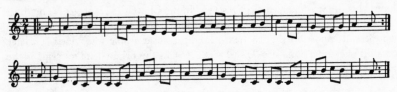

5. SHUFFLING SONG

An early shuffling song in slow $\frac{3}{4}$ time, three paces forward, three back, etc. Like the preceding wordless tunes, this song was hummed, intoned or sung to various syllables. From a New Lebanon manuscript of the early 1790's.

6. THE HAPPY JOURNEY

"The Happy Journey," the first Shaker hymn with notes, was written at the Watervliet community in 1807, and sung at New Lebanon, Hancock, Harvard and probably other societies the same year. The second line of the first verse was one of those frank but symbolic statements seized upon by the world as evidence of "immoral" behavior.

The tune, found in an old manuscript, was an early Shaker "solemn song;" the words (eleven verses) were published in Millennial Praises (1813), pp. 121-2. Suggested key for singing: C minor. The time would be Largo, in the Shaker sense; Moderato, or better still, Allegretto, in the modern designation.

O the hap-py jour-ney that we are pur-su-ing, Come breth-ren and sis-ters let's all strip to run. Let all be a-wak-ened and up and be do-ing That we may at-tain to our des-tin-ed home.

2. The heavens of glory is our destination
   We're swiftly advancing to that happy shore;
   We're travelling on in the regeneration,
   And when we get through we shall sorrow no more.

3. This beautiful journey which we've undertaken,
   Excels all the travel that ever has been,
   And those that perform it will never be shaken,
   Because it leads out of the nature of sin.

7. A PEOPLE CALLED CHRISTIANS

The words and tune of this song are almost identical with those of "Spiritual Sailor," which appeared in the "Southern Harmony" in 1835. (See Jackson, "Spiritual Folk-Songs of Early America," No. 136.) Did William Walker, the compiler of that hymnal, take the text from the Shakers' "Millennial Praises" (1813), or did the text in each book originate in some common source? The tune here used, from Haskell's "Musical Expositor" (p. 80), is undoubtedly a borrowing; Dr. Jackson calls the same tune, the one to which "Spiritual Sailor" was set, "a close variant of 'When the Stormy Winds do Blow' or 'You Gentlemen of England', a song of seafaring which appears to have been widely sung in England over a long period." (Op. cit., p. 155.)

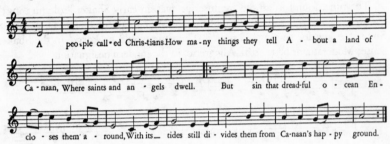

A peo-ple call-ed Chris-tians.How ma-ny things they tell A - bout a land of Ca - naan, Where saints and an - gels dwell. But sin that dread-ful o - cean En-clo - ses them a - round,With its— tides still di - vides them from Ca-naan's hap - py ground.

8. THE HUMBLE HEART

One of the earliest hymns to be supplied with notes. From the George De Witt hymnal, New Lebanon, 1822.

1. Whence comes this bright ce - les - tial light, What cause pro - duc - es this, A heav-en o - pens to my sight, Bright scenes of joy and bliss. O Lord Je - ho - vah art Thou here, This light pro - claims Thou art, I am in - deed, I'm al - ways near Un - to the hum - ble heart.

FIG. 15.—In 1870, after Elder Frederick Evans, the "public preacher" of the Lebanon community, had completed an historic mission to England, The London Graphic commissioned A. Boyd Houghton to do a series of drawings of the American Shakers. "The Final Procession," the title of the present print, depicts a solemn march at the close of a meeting, with the hands of the worshippers uplifted to receive God's blessing. The tall figure at the right is Elder Frederick himself.

FIG. 16.—Like the second meeting-house at New Lebanon, the second church at Watervliet had a vaulted ceiling. The suspended rods may be the frames of sounding-boards. Sitting on the benches are the aged and infirm who could not participate in the lively "wheel" dance here portrayed. The title of the picture is "The Shakers in Niskeyuna-Religious Exercises."

2. The proud and lofty I despise,
   And bless the meek and low,
   I hear the humble soul that cries,
   And comfort I bestow.
   Of all the trees among the wood
   I've chose one little vine,
   The meek and low are nigh to me,
   The humble heart is mine.

3. Tall cedars fall before the wind,
   The tempest breaks the oak,
   While slender vines will bow & bend
   And rise beneath the stroke.
   I've chosen me one pleasant grove
   And set my lovely vine,
   Here in my vineyard I will rove,
   The humble heart is mine.

4. Of all the fowls that beat the air
   I've chose one little dove,
   I've made her spotless white & fair,
   The object of my love.
   Her feathers are like purest gold,
   With glory she does shine,
   She is a beauty to behold,
   Her humble heart is mine.

5. Of all the kinds that range at large
   I've chose one little flock,
   And those I make my lovely charge,
   Before them I will walk.
   Their constant shepherd I will be,
   And all their ways refine,
   And they shall serve & rev'rence me,
   The humble heart is mine.

[101]

6. Of all the sects that fill the land
   One little band I've chose,
   And led them forth by my right hand
   And plac'd my love on those.
   The lovely object of my love,
   Around my heart shall twine
   My flock, my vineyard & my dove,
   The humble heart is mine.

9. FUNERAL HYMN

An early funeral hymn, which should be sung slowly and solemnly. Key, E minor. From the George DeWitt hymnal, New Lebanon, 1822.

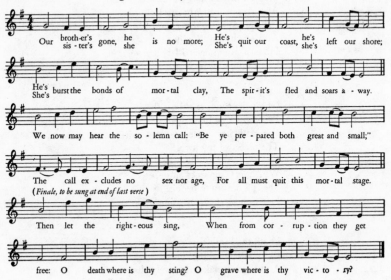

Our broth-er's sis-ter's gone, he she is no more; He's She's quit our coast, he's she's left our shore;

He's She's burst the bonds of mor-tal clay, The spir-it's fled and soars a-way.

We now may hear the so-lemn call: "Be ye pre-pared both great and small;"

The call ex-cludes no sex nor age, For all must quit this mor-tal stage.

(*Finale, to be sung at end of last verse*)

Then let the right-eous sing, When from cor-rup-tion they get

free: O death where is thy sting? O grave where is thy vic-to-ry?

10. COME LIFE, SHAKER LIFE

Where and when this well-known Shaker song was written, no one knows. Apparently it came out of one of the western communes at an early period and was widely sung: though, strangely enough, it was included in only one of the hundreds of eastern hymnals which the author has examined. "Come life" was a spirited dance, accompanied by shaking motions and ending abruptly. In another version the text reads:

> Shake, shake along, shake along, Daniel,
> Shake, shake out of me all things carnal.

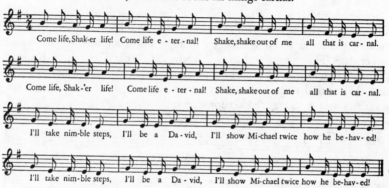

11. ONE, TWO, THREE STEPS

Because this song was used as an aid in dancing the square order shuffle, it appears in the hymnals of many societies. Though the present version is from an Enfield, Conn. manuscript dated March 8, 1852, the tune is much earlier. It is definitely "Irish" in feeling, with a jogging, two-beats-to-the-measure pace. Suggested speed, ♩.=106.

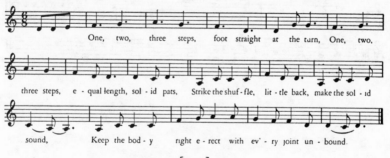

12. COME MOTHER'S SONS AND DAUGHTERS

A western Shaker song first sung by Elder Issachar Bates, Sen'r, one of the three missionaries who carried the gospel into Ohio and Kentucky. Recorded by Henry DeWitt at New Lebanon in 1837, words and melody are both of earlier date. The tune is probably derivative: cf. "Rose Tree," from Knoxville (Tenn.) Harmony, in "Spiritual Folk-Songs of Early America" (Jackson). Note how the metrical pattern changes with each section; in the fourth section $\frac{4}{4}$ alternates with $\frac{4}{3}$. Suggested key for singing: G—first note B.

13. SOLEMN SONG

This piece, composed at the Hill family, New Lebanon, in 1838, is patterned after the solemn "noted" songs of early Shaker history. It has a stately character, more dignified than "solemn." H. DeWitt MS. The original form of notation is retained, though the song is an interesting example of a true $\frac{5}{4}$ meter. Speed: Shaker Adagio ($\textit{J}$=80).

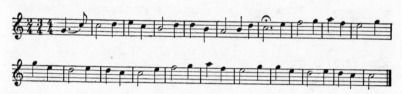

14. SQUARE ORDER SHUFFLE

From Isaac N. Youngs' "A Short Abridgement of the Rules of Music" (p. 37). Written in "compound mode, sub-measure," two beats to the measure, and hummed or chanted at a speed of $\textit{♪}$.=90-100. Square order shuffle time, according to Youngs, is about 122 swings a minute of a weighted string 9½ inches long. The pentatonic, 5-tone scale is here employed.

15. O THE SIMPLE GIFTS OF GOD

Probably a square order shuffle song. It was sent by Polly Champlain, of North Union, Ohio—where it originated—to Luther C. (Copley) of New Lebanon, and recorded by Mary Hazzard in one of her hymnals. (n.d.) The time is in modal minor, like the old English or Scotch folk-songs. The speed, Allegro Vivace ($\downarrow$=c. 108). Suggested key for singing, F minor, starting on middle C.

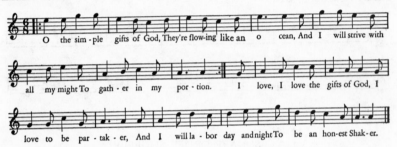

O the sim-ple gifts of God, They're flow-ing like an o cean, And I will strive with all my might To gath-er in my por-tion. I love, I love the gifts of God, I love to be par-tak-er, And I will la-bor day and night To be an hon-est Shak-er.

16. HOLY ORDER

The forward-and-backward, square order dance devised by Father Joseph Meacham is demonstrated in this product of a "chain" of inspiration. "The above song," the MS. reads, "is one that Mother Ann sang to Father Joseph when he had the gift of labouring in square order. Elder Sister Olive [a beloved eldress who had died some years before] sang it to Semantha F. [Semantha Fairbanks, an instrument] for she knew that we had wanted to know how Father got the gift of Labouring. July 12th, 1839." A slow, solemn song typical of the early mode of worship.

Step on, turn a-round, Back and turn in or-der, Step on se len ven ve In ho-ly or-der. For-ward go se len ven vo, Back in ho-ly or-der.

17. MARCHING TUNE

From Isaac N. Youngs' "A Short Abridgement of the Rules of Music," p. 37.
A tune with more shape and form than many Shaker pieces: note that the 4th,
8th, 12th and 16th are cadence measures giving a rhythmic balance to the
melody. Allegro ($\quarternote=106$).

18. I'VE SET MY FACE FOR ZION'S KINGDOM

A brisk marching song, to be sung with a will. The manuscript gives the
date as January, 1850, but not the source. Probably New Lebanon.

19. WAKE UP STUR ABOUT

A lively round dance composed by Sarah Ann Van Vyke at the New Lebanon East (or Hill) family on Jan. 2, 1847. From a New Lebanon hymnal. The Shaker "allegro" should be designated in this case as ♪=about 106.

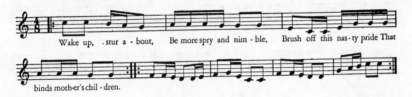

Wake up, stur a - bout, Be more spry and nim - ble, Brush off this nas-ty pride That

binds moth-er's chil - dren.

20. LIKE PRETTY BIRDS

A "merry" round dance "from the west," some time in the 1840's. Mary Hazzard MS. Moderate speed.

Like pret - ty birds a - mong the trees I will be all in mo - tion, And

sing and skip up - on the breeze Of love and sweet de - vo - tion.

For lo it is a hap - py time, A time of mak - ing mer - ry, Of

heaven-ly com - forts all di - vine And ver - y cheer - ing, ver - y.

21. COME DANCE AND SING

A spirited round dance: the last part is in the nature of a refrain, to be sung with increased animation. This song is attributed, by the visionist who "received" it in 1838, to the spirit of Issachar Bates, Sr., who had died the preceding year.

22. I HAVE A LITTLE UNION BELL

A merry little dance, to be sung to a lively tempo. Typical of the make-believe or play-songs of the great Shaker revival. Source unknown, possibly Canterbury or Tyringham about 1849.

23. O I LOVE MOTHER

A stirring dance song, to be sung zestfully. Found in a collection with no dates or sources given, but probably from New Lebanon or Hancock about 1847.

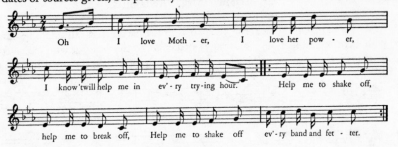

24. TURNING SONG

A cheerful, lively dance during which the worshippers constantly turned or whirled. (New Lebanon, May 16, 1844.) In a similar song from Tyringham (1850) the singers turned around four times, or kept turning while they counted four:

> "I'll turn turn around,
> One, two, three, four,
> To gain holy power,
> For I want more and more."

This verse was repeated over and over, with a short wordless tune between. The New Lebanon turning song may be sung in the key of A or A flat, the first tone C♯ or C.

25. AWAKE MY SOUL

A lively song, again on the "Yankee Doodle" order, which came "From the west," probably the South Union, Ky., society. Taken from a New Lebanon manuscript. The Shaker time designation is "sub-allegro." Suggested speed, ♪=106.

A - wake my soul a - rise and shake, No time to ev - er pon - der,

Keep a - wake, keep a - wake Lest ye be rent a - sun - der.

I will be good, I will be free, I'll hate the old de - ceiv - er, No

earth - ly tie shall fet - ter me, I'll be a good be - liev - er.

26. LOVE, LOVE, LOVE

This song was recorded at the Enfield (Conn.) community on October 26, 1851. The tune is that of the old German folk-song, "Hop, Hop, Hop, Hop my Birdie Hop." The Shaker Largo (♩=91) is a becoming speed. Wavy lines over certain passages in the original MS. probably indicate trills.

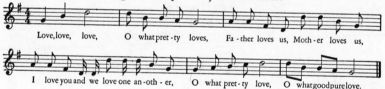

Love, love, love, O what pret -ty loves, Fa - ther loves us, Moth - er loves us,

I love you and we love one an -oth - er, O what pret - ty love, O what good pure love.

27. FOLLOWERS OF THE LAMB

A rather lively song from the manuscript hymnal of Clarissa Jacobs, Second family, New Lebanon. Dated 1847. Cf. "My Bible Leads to Glory," No. 233 in "Spiritual Folk Songs of Early America." (Jackson)

"O Brethren ain't you happy" and "Take my hands in brotherly love" (p. 151) are exceptional in the fact that they stem directly from, or are closely related in structure to early American religious or revival folk-songs. Examples of songs with the first line repeated three times and followed by a one-line variant are common among the negro and white spirituals. Though Shaker songs constructed with a recurrent fourth line or "chorus" are rare, many pieces, especially the one-line repeated songs, indicate revival origin.

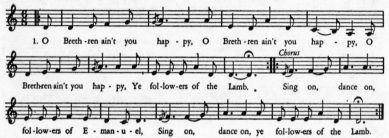

1. O Breth-ren ain't you hap-py, O Breth-ren ain't you hap-py, O Breth-ren ain't you hap-py, Ye fol-low-ers of the Lamb.

Chorus

Sing on, dance on, fol-low-ers of E-man-u-el, Sing on, dance on, ye fol-low-ers of the Lamb.

2. O Sisters ain't you happy,
O Sisters ain't you happy,
O Sisters ain't you happy,
Ye followers of the Lamb.

Chorus:
Sing on, dance on, etc.

3. I'm glad I am a shaker,
I'm glad I am a shaker,
I'm glad I am a shaker,
Ye followers of the Lamb.

Chorus:
Sing on, dance on, etc.

4. I mean to be obedient,
I mean to be obedient,
I mean to be obedient,
Ye followers of the Lamb.

Chorus:
Sing on, dance on, etc.

28. QUICK DANCE

A typical quick dance tune, such as the worshippers hummed or otherwise articulated in their fast-paced circular dances. Vivace. The manuscript hymnals of the sect include many "noted" (wordless) songs: quick dances, step tunes, standing songs, marches, round dances, etc. etc. This particular number is from the first bishopric (New Lebanon, Watervliet and Groveland) about 1848.

29. I WILL BOW AND BE SIMPLE

A "bowing song" from the North family, New Lebanon, recorded by Mary Hazzard in 1847. The tune sounds well when sung in the key of E flat. Suggested speed, ♩=91.

In Shaker speech, "yea" is pronounced "ye" (ē as in greet).

I will bow and be sim-ple, I . will bow and be free, I will bow and be hum-ble, Yea bow 'like the wil-low tree. I will bow this is the to-ken, I will wear the eas-y yoke, I will bow and be bro-ken, Yea I'll fall up-on the rock.

30. WHO WILL BOW AND BEND LIKE A WILLOW

Originating about 1843 at the Canterbury community, this song appears to have spread to many other societies. It is included, sometimes under the title of "Laughing John's Interrogatory," in several New Lebanon hymnals. "Laughing John" was a "simple-minded" spirit manifested in a medium who, strangely, "was not especially of a mirthful turn of mind. . . The laugh, however, as silly as it may have been, was passed from one to another, till the whole body, young and old, would burst out with one merry peal of laughter." (Blinn: The Manifestation of Spiritualism among the Shakers, p. 51.) The tune has something of the quality of a negro spiritual.

The piece is fairly brisk, sub-allegro ($\quarternote$=106) in the Shaker designation.

Who will bow and bend like a wil-low, Who will turn and twist and reel

In the gale of sim-ple free-dom, From the bower of un-ion flow-ing.

Who will drink the wine of pow-er, Drop-ping down like a show-er,

Pride and bond-age all for-get-ting, Moth-er's wine is free-ly work-ing.

Oh ho! I will have it, I will bow and bend to get it,

I'll be reel-ing, turn-ing, twist-ing, Shake out all the starch and stiff'-ning!

31. SHAKE OFF THE FLESH

A typical shaking and warring-against-the-flesh song of the great Shaker revival. Source and exact date unknown. Moderato.

Come, let us all u-nite To purge out this filth-y, flesh-y, car-nal sense, And la-bor for the pow-er of God To mor-ti-fy and stain our pride. We'll raise our glitt'-ring swords and fight. And war the flesh with all our might, All car-nal ties we now will break And in the pow'r of God we'll shake. God we'll shake.

32. HOP UP AND JUMP UP

A popular revival song from Pleasant Garden (Shirley) about 1847. Rather lively, and originally accompanied by the motions and gestures indicated. From one of Mary Hazzard's hymnals, New Lebanon.

Hop up and jump up and whirl round, whirl round, Gath-er love, here it is, all round, all round. Here is love flow-ing round, catch it as you whirl round, Reach up and reach down, here it is all round.

33. VISION SONG

"Heard in vision" and presumably sung in a trance by Clarissa Shoefelt, a young sister at the Gathering Order, Watervliet. The time was October, 1837, soon after the outbreak of the great Shaker revival. Words and tune were transcribed soon after reception. The present version is from Henry DeWitt's New Lebanon hymnal, begun the above year.

The variations in meter may represent the attempt, on the part of the "score-pricker," to give a literal rendering of words and tones which must have been irregularly expressed. Speed, the Shaker Largo (♩=91). Suggested key for singing, A flat, starting on E flat (with grace note) above middle C.

How hap-py pret-ty lit-tle an-gels are, O how hap - py!

34. MOTHER SAYS GO ON DEAR CHILDREN

One of the first "vision songs" recorded at the Watervliet or Niskeyuna community. Sung by Matilda Southwick in October, 1837, the text is brief, as usual in this type. Such songs were often extended by repetition, the addition of a few wordless measures, or both. "Mother says" was probably sung joyously and with ardour, in the spirit of a triumphal march.

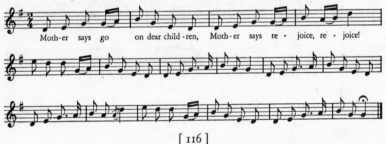

Moth-er says go on dear child-ren, Moth-er says re - joice, re - joice!

Fig. 17.—An evening meeting by lamp-light.

35. O SAN-NISK-A-NA

A "vision song" in "unknown tongue" by Laura Sheperdson, the East or Hill family, New Lebanon, ca. 1838. Henry DeWitt MS. Presto (♪=128-160).

O san‑nisk‑a‑na   nisk‑a‑na,   haw, haw, haw, fan‑nick‑a‑na   nisk‑a‑na,   haw, haw, haw.

O san‑nisk‑a‑na,   nisk‑a‑na   yea se‑ne‑aw,   fan‑a‑na,   nisk‑a‑na,   haw, haw, haw.

O san‑nisk‑a‑ṅa‑na,   haw, haw, fan‑nik‑a‑na‑na,   haw, haw,   O sen‑a‑go fan‑

a, nick‑a‑na‑ná   na nick‑a‑na‑na   O sen‑a‑go fan‑ a, nick‑a‑na‑na na.

36. MOTHER ANN'S SONG

Note that Mother Ann herself did not sing this song, but that it was received from her spirit. Cf. No. 1. The DeWitt MS. reads: "Learned of Mother Ann. Sept. 22nd 1844. (O. W.)" It is one of numerous "vive vum" songs, lively in sound and effect—like the rhythm of drum beats—but with a rather slow pulse. Cf. the old song, "Ve, vi, vo, vum, I smell the blood, etc." (Shaker Adagio (♩=80) is about the correct speed.

Vum vi‑ve vum vi‑ve   vum vum vo,   Ve vum vi‑ve vum vi‑ve   vum vum vo,

Vum vi‑ve vum vi‑ve   vum vum vo,   Ve vum vi‑ve vo   ve vum vum vo.

Vum vi‑ve vum vi‑ve   vum vum vo,   Vi‑ve vi‑ve vi‑ve vi‑ve vum vum vo,

Vum vi‑ve vum vi‑ve   vum vum vo, Ve vum vi‑ve vum ve vum vum vo.

37. FROM THE MOON

A characteristic "vision song" in unknown tongues. The Shakers developed a remarkable facility in singing this doggerel, which follows, in the record at least, a definite rhythmic pattern. At the end of the score the scribe has written: "The above song was learned in vision by one of the sisters at Groveland (N. Y.) while visiting the moon." Date, probably Sept., 1838. Occasionally these songs in strange tongues were followed by an "interpretation." (See p. 76.)

Se - le - i as - ka - na va, Ves - e - ven ve - ne vi, Ve - le - o as - ka - na fa, Fe - ne - es

veen fe - ne fi. Ve - se - fa ve - ne - fa ve - ne fen - ne fenne fi, Va - se - fa va - se - fa veen fen - ne fi.

O, ho ho ho! Oh, ho ho ho! Oh, ho ho ho! Haw ew oh hoo hoo, aw ew aw hoo hoo.

Aw ew aw, ew ew oh, ho - a oh - a, oh - a ho, Aw ew aw, ew oh oh, ho oh - a oo.

38. INE VINE VIOLET

A characteristic example of the nonsense rhyme of which the Shakers were so fond during their exciting revivals. This vivacious number was composed by Hannah Ann Agnew, a New Lebanon instrument, in 1838.

I - ne vi - ne vi - o - let, E - ne se - ne vin - go pret, Y - fen wa - fen

wa - ne voo, O - le mo - le min - zy two A - cren wa - cren wa - ney vo,

Moth - er s love is e - ven so, U - ne e - ne I - ne va, Now in love we'll dance and play.

<h1>Tunes and Music</h1>

39. LAY ME LOW

A "gift song" received by Addah Z. Potter of the New Lebanon Church order on April 15, 1838. One of many songs of humility and "mortification" written during the manifestations, this piece has a curious American Indian quality, slow, soft and plaintive. The tune is modal.

Lay me low, Lay me low, Lay me low, low Where

Moth-er can find me, Where Moth-er can own me, Where Moth-er can bless me.

40. LUCY CLARK'S EXALTATION

One of the strange ejaculatory songs of the instruments while under the influence of inspiration. Such songs were given musical form after the event, either by the singer or by a recorder versed in musical writing. Under the score, in the DeWitt MS., is the following explanation: "Sung by Lucy Clark in our Sab. afternoon meeting; when all attended that had died within twenty years. She walked around sister Betsy B. with her hands raised and sung this song in the sublime raptures of joy for her privilege to attend meeting with her dear companions. Feb. 23rd, 1840."

Oh heav-en of heav-ens, the bless-ings of heav-en are free! Oh

heav-en of heav-en, 'tis heav-en of heav-ens to me!

[119]

41. I HAVE A LITTLE DRUM

A gift-song from the Shirley society. The gift was a "drum," whose beat may be distinguished in the second part of the song. About 1850. Mary Hazzard hymnal. Moderate speed.

I have a lit-tle drum that Moth-er gave to me, The pret-tiest lit-tle drum that ev-er you did see. I'll drum night and day, I'll drum night and day, To call vol-un-teers to fight sin a-way.

42. MOTHER'S LOVE

A gay "Indian" song from the Second family in New Lebanon. Clarissa Jacobs manuscript, 1847. The final "shout" often occurred in, though it was not confined to the "racial" songs. Tempo, ♩=106. The song may be sung in the key of E flat, with B flat as the first tone.

Jump take Moth-er's love, Me bring it free-ly, From the shin-y worlds a-bove. See it spar-kle clear-ly. *Shout*

43. ME BLESS THE CROSS

Another "Indian" song, this one "given" at Holy Ground (Canterbury) on June 17, 1847. From a Mary Hazzard hymnal dated the same year. The correct speed, ♩=128-160, is the Shaker even mode presto. In the original manuscript the time signatures alternate between $\frac{2}{4}$ and $\frac{3}{4}$ throughout the piece.

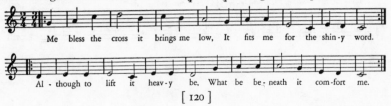

Me bless the cross it brings me low, It fits me for the shin-y word. Al-though to lift it heav-y be, What be be-neath it com-fort me.

44. THIS BE DE WAY

An "Indian" song from the South family, New Lebanon. (n.d.) Sung gaily and with appropriate gestures. Mary Hazzard MS.

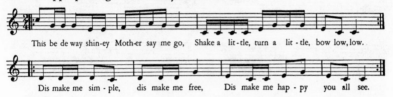

This be de way shin-ey Moth-er say me go, Shake a lit-tle, turn a lit-tle, bow low, low.

Dis make me sim-ple, dis make me free, Dis make me hap-py you all see.

45. BLACK BILL'S WONDERMENT

A "negro" "drinking" song from the Second family, Canterbury, first sung on Feb. 22, 1847. Not to be sung too fast; the Shaker speed is allegro.

Why I won-der you don't laugh a lit-tle, Laugh a lit-tle and laugh a lit-tle,

Why I won-der you aint all reel-ing, Back-wards, for-wards, side-ways and down-ward.

Why I won-der you can go so straight And keep such a slick and

cu-ri-ous shape, For of Moth-er's wine I've got a small por-tion And it

sets me in-to a stag-g'ring mo-tion Well, well, I'm will-ing to stag-ger,

Stag-ger, stag-ger a-way from bon-dage, Well, well, I'm

will-ing to reel, Reel, reel, reel in-to free-dom.

[121]

46. AN INDIAN SONG

Another "vision song" from Groveland. 1838. Moderate speed.

47. "TURK" SONG

A racial song "sent to Sarah J. Rea by R. B." (New Lebanon?) in 1843. Speed, ♩=91, Shaker allegro. Suggested key for singing, D, with A as the first note.

48. CHINESE

A racial vision song, also from Groveland. (n.d.) Note the inclusion of the three English words. Not too fast.

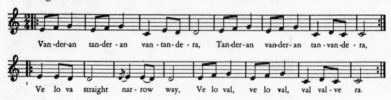

49. SONG OF CO-LO-VIN

A "bird" song, New Lebanon, Oct. 8, 1839. (See p. 28.) Henry DeWitt, the compiler, wrote at the end of the score: "Sung by a little bird of Paradise (Co-lo-vin by name) that came to see its mate, which was sent to Elder Sister and Betsy Bates with a song some days before."

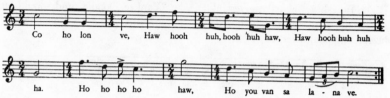

50. I'M A SCOTCH BONNY WEE ONE

A "Scotch" song from Holy Ground (Canterbury) about 1847. Though belonging in the same category as the "Indian," "Chinese," "Hottentot" and other native or racial compositions, this piece represents a more serious attempt to catch the dialect. To be sung in a rather lively manner (Shaker allegro, compound mode), but not too fast.

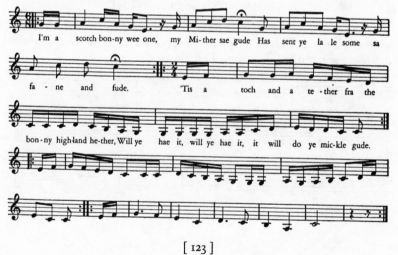

51. DRINK YE OF MOTHER'S WINE

A "drinking" song popular with the Shakers and appearing in many collections. Cf. Nos. 45 and 52. "The Gift of spiritual wine carried a great evidence of its reality, by the paroxysms of intoxication which it produced, causing those who drank it to stagger and reel like drunken people." (Isaac N. Youngs MS.)

The tune bears a striking resemblance to "Yankee Doodle" and should be sung at the same speed (about ♪=106). The present version is from a Mary Hazzard hymnal dated 1847.

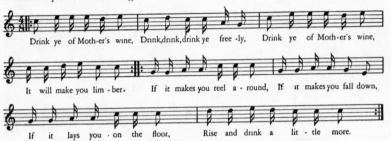

Drink ye of Mother's wine, Drink, drink, drink ye free-ly, Drink ye of Mother's wine,

It will make you lim-ber. If it makes you reel a-round, If it makes you fall down,

If it lays you on the floor, Rise and drink a lit-tle more.

52. HOLY MOTHER GIVE TO ME

A "drinking song" from Pleasant Hill, Ky., sent to Sister Lucy Smith of New Lebanon and recorded in hymnals at Holy Mount. The speed is allegro (♪=106). Suggested key for singing, F starting with F.

Ho-ly Moth-er give to me A pret-ty lit-tle cup for thee,

Fill'd with wine, pur-est wine, Take the cup and drink it up!

O Ho! O Ho! I love Mother's wine, O Ho! O Ho! I'll drink ev'-ry time.

53. SWEEP, SWEEP AND CLEANSE YOUR FLOOR

A slow, impressive ritual song whose tune has modal attributes. In the New Lebanon hymnal from which this version was taken, the song is attributed to Eleanor Potter; date of composition, March 27, 1839. Shaker Largo ($\quarternote$=91). The song may be sung in D major, with A as the first note.

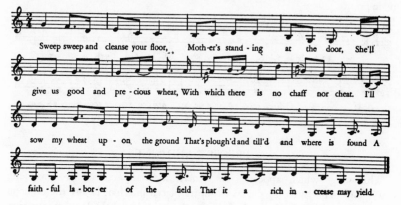

Sweep sweep and cleanse your floor, Moth-er's stand - ing at the door, She'll give us good and pre - cious wheat, With which there is no chaff nor cheat. I'll sow my wheat up - on the ground That's plough'd and till'd and where is found A faith - ful la - bor - er of the field That it a rich in - crease may yield.

54. SCOUR AND SCRUB

Another ritual song, first performed at New Lebanon in December, 1841. From Henry DeWitt's "Collection of Songs of Various Kinds," New Lebanon. A slow song of mortification; the speed, adagio.

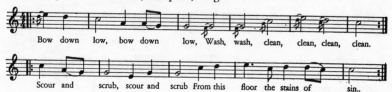

Bow down low, bow down low, Wash, wash, clean, clean, clean, clean. Scour and scrub, scour and scrub From this floor the stains of sin..

55. DISMISSION OF THE DEVIL

An interesting tune of odd measure construction, with a queer fitting of words. This "warring" song, which probably originated in the Harvard or Shirley community, was widely sung throughout the order. To be singable, the speed should be designated as ♩.=about 91. The Shaker signature is compound mode presto.

Be joy-ful, be joy-ful. be joy-ful, be joy - ful, For Old Ug-ly is go - ing.

Good rid-dance, good rid-dance, good rid-dance we say, And don't you nev-er come here a - gain.

56. PRECEPT AND LINE

This song—which appears, like others, in many collections—was sung slowly and deliberately as the worshippers placed one foot before the other in "the narrow path." At the end of the score, in the Henry DeWitt manuscript, is the legend: "Given by Father James, to be sung for to exercise the narrow path. November 4th, 1840." The song is modal.

Pre - cept on pre - cept and line up - on line,

We'll walk in the path our

Moth - er has trod, Yea straight and clear straight-ness, the pure way of God.

57. THE VOICE OF GOD

A ritual song (see text) with a vigorous driving quality, as would be expected from the nature of the rite. The recorder, Henry DeWitt, wrote at the end of the score: "Words spoken by the Lord Nov'r 28, 1841 at our supper table." The speed should be Shaker Largo (♩=91) or Allegro (♩=106). Suggested key for singing, A, with E as the first note.

I will roar, roar, roar, I will roar, roar, roar, Yea and I'll howl, howl, howl in my fu - ry, saith the Lord, Be cause of the a bom - i - na - tion that rests in my Zi - on. And I will send forth a curse, curse, curse; Yea I will send forth a heav - y curse, Up - on the in - hab - i - tants that dwell in her.

58. SEARCH YE YOUR CAMPS

Sung annually for many years to accompany the ritual of purification. (See text.) Appearing in many hymnals, the song is here transcribed from the De Witt MS., with its legend: "Given by Father William, Dec. 16, 1841. New Lebanon." The $\frac{3}{4}$ $\frac{2}{4}$ in the time signature seems the best way to express the alternation of triple and duple meter. Suggested speed, largo ($\downarrow$=91); suggested key for singing, F, beginning with C (and grace note).

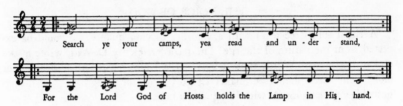

Search ye your camps, yea read and un-der-stand,

For the Lord God of Hosts holds the Lamp in His hand.

59: SWEEP AS I GO

A sweeping-ritual song written in September, 1840, by Elder Abraham Perkins of the Enfield (N. H.) Church. Henry DeWitt MS. The speed should approximate the normal rhythm of a person sweeping as he walks along, not too slow, not too fast. In a sense, this is a true work-song, certainly a song expressive of religious labour.

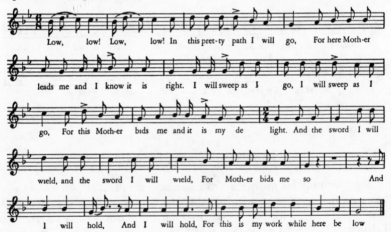

Low, low! Low, low! In this pret-ty path I will go, For here Moth-er

leads me and I know it is right. I will sweep as I go, I will sweep as I

go, For this Moth-er bids me and it is my de light. And the sword I will

wield, and the sword I will wield, For Moth-er bids me so And

I will hold, And I will hold, For this is my work while here be low

60. WHEN CHEER FILLS THE HEARTS OF MY FRIENDS

An example of the assembling of text and tune. The words were written at Holy Ground (Canterbury) by B. J. K.; the tune came from Harvard. The completed "hymn," known as "Kindness and Love," was recorded at Enfield, Conn., Jan. 18, 1852. The signature in the original is compound mode, largo, or 122 beats to a minute. Suggested speed, 60 to the dotted quarter (♩.=60); suggested key, G.

When cheer fills the hearts of my friends And breth-ren and sis - ters are kind, What joy to my bo - som it sends, What peace to my troub - led mind. To know that my dear gos - pel kin Have love and af - fec - tion for me, My spir - it from sor - row does win And caus - es de - jec - tion to flee.

61. STEP TUNE

In "step" tunes or "walking" tunes, the step was a walk or shuffle, not the springing gait or lope of most dances. The above number was recorded at the First or Church Order, New Lebanon, about 1858. A reasonable speed would be ♩=106. The tune may properly be played in the key of B flat.

62. A MINCE PIE OR A PUDING

A cheerful little "welcome" song with a light-hearted cadence, one of many used in the Shaker families to welcome friends, especially visitors in the eldership or ministry. The Shaker speed is "sub-allegro." Source: New Lebanon.

Wel-come here, Wel-come here, All be a - live And be of good cheir.

I've got a pie All baked com - plete, And pud - ing too that's ver - y sweet.

63. MY CARNAL LIFE I WILL LAY DOWN

This song, from South Union, Ky., dated June, 1838, appears to have been confined chiefly to the western Shakers; it has come to light only once in the hymnals of the northeast. Differing from the uni-tonality of most Shaker tunes, "My carnal life" shows signs of a modulation to C major in the first two bars of the second part, shifting thereafter back to the original A minor. To be sung at a moderate speed. Suggested key for singing: F minor, starting with F.

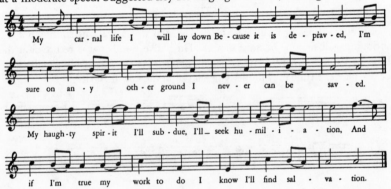

My car - nal life I will lay down Be - cause it is de - praved, I'm sure on an - y oth - er ground I nev - er can be sav - ed. My haugh - ty spir - it I'll sub - due, I'll seek hu - mil - i - a - tion, And if I'm true my work to do I know I'll find sal - va - tion.

64. SHEPHERDESS SONG

"Brought by the shepherdess to the Second Order (New Lebanon) Feb. 8, 1844." In the first two months of this year many songs were received from a mythical keeper of sheep in the celestial pastures. New Lebanon hymnal. The tune is very rhythmical, with a noticeably strong accent on the down beat of every measure. The Shaker "allegro" for this song should be rendered as ♩=91. The key of A, beginning on A, is suggested for singing.

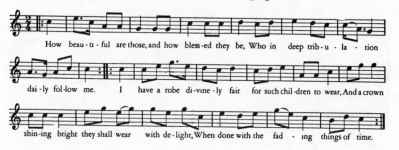

65. NOW MY DEAR COMPANIONS

Once in a great while, in the Shaker hymnals, there appears a song in three or four-part harmony, experimental compositions which anticipate the music written after 1870. This piece, with its treble, tenor and base parts, is from the hymnal of A. P. B. (Augustus P. Blase) who was one of the most prolific song-writers at the Watervliet (N. Y.) community. It was probably written about the time of the Civil War. Included in the same manuscript is a four-part song, "I'll be an angel of mercy," whose parts are designated tenor, alto, air and base.

1. Now, my dear companions, is the time to start anew, A-new,
a-new, for the kingdom of Heaven. With faith and zeal and courage strong,
we will ever be marching on, Toiling on, struggling on, for a perfect Heaven.

2. We will not be hindered while we walk the narrow way,
Narrow way, narrow way, with our gospel kindred.
But every foe that comes in view, in ourselves we will subdue,
And be true to subdue the way that leads to glory.

[132]

66. OH THE BEAUTIFUL TREASURES

An Enfield (N. H.) song of the year 1849.

O the beau-ti-ful trea-sure laid up for the wise, How pre-cious the val-ue, how glo-ri-ous the prize. O the beau-ti-ful trea-sure laid up for the wise, How pre-cious the val-ue, how glo-ri-ous the prize. Far bright-er than dia-monds on prin-ce's brow And rich-er than roy-al-ty can be-stow. Far bright-er than dia-monds on prin-ce's brow And rich-er than roy-al-ty can be-stow.

67. THE BUGLE

An imitation of a bugle call as "received from Daniel's (Daniel Boler's) Bugle" by an unnamed instrument. Time, the Sabbath, April 14, 1839. From the Henry DeWitt manuscript. Suggested speed, moderato; key, A, with E as the first note.

O ho ho ho, O ho ho ho, O ho ho ho.

68. LITTLE TRUMPET

"Little Trumpet" was brought east from the Union Village, Ohio, community, where it was written in November, 1840. From the Henry DeWitt collection. Like the "Bugle" songs and the White Water piece which begins— "Blow ye, blow ye, blow ye the trumpet, toot, toot, toot"—it apparently attempts to simulate a musical instrument. A moderate speed, such as the Shaker Largo (♩=91) is fitting.

O this pret-ty lit-tle trum-pet I will blow, O it is from the heav-ens I do know.

I'll blow, blow my trum-pet, toot, toot, toot, I'll blow my trum-pet, toot, toot.

69. LOVE AND BLESSING

A "spelling-out" song. From the DeWitt MS. we learn that the piece was sent "from Mother Lucy to the Elders brethren and sisters, for their being willing to pray for the Believers at Watervliet and elsewhere. Oct. 19th, 1839." To be sung at a moderately slow tempo. Suggested key for singing, F, starting with F above middle C.

M o t h e r-s e n d s-h e r-l o v e-a n d-b le

s s i n g-T o-c o m f o r t-a n-d s-t r e n g t

h e n-a l l. Moth-er sends her love and bles-sing To com-fort and strength-en all.

70. LET ME HAVE MOTHER'S GOSPEL

A favorite song at the Hancock community, found in one of the early hymnals of that society. (n.d.) The late Sister Alice Smith documented the song as follows: "The above was often used when we 'faced in;' all would sing and walk around, imparting love by waving hands and clasping hands." It is a cheerful ditty, with a fairly fast tempo.

Let me have Moth-er's gos-pel, Moth-er's soul sav-ing gos-pel, The same life that she taught, that she lived in her day. Free from all that is car-nal, breath-ing life, life e-ter-nal, From the world, from the flesh 'tis a-way, far a-way.

71. MOTHER LUCY'S BIRTHDAY SONG

"Sung by Mother Lucy [i.e. her spirit] to the Elder Sisters Feby 5th 1841." DeWitt MS. Had she lived, Mother Ann's successor "in the female line" would have been eighty-one years old on the above date. A cheerful song, to be sung at a spirited pace.

O my be-lov-ed Ka-re-ne-va-ne, Will ye re-ceive this love to-day, For I have love and so have you And we will mix it through and through. For tru-ly 'tis the love of Moth-er And I do know you want no oth-er, And when this day is past and gone, It then will leave me eight-y one!

72. SIMPLE GIFTS

Like "Come life, Shaker life," this song was sung everywhere in the United Society. It appears in many collections copied down during the period of "Mother Ann's Work" (1837-1847 and after) and probably was a product of that revival. One manuscript states that the song was "composed by the Alfred Ministry June 28, 1848." It is a rather lively piece, Shaker Allegro in the original MS.

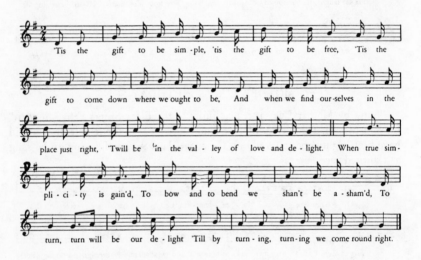

'Tis the gift to be sim-ple, 'tis the gift to be free, 'Tis the gift to come down where we ought to be, And when we find our-selves in the place just right, 'Twill be 'in the val-ley of love and de-light. When true sim-pli-ci-ty is gain'd, To bow and to bend we shan't be a-sham'd, To turn, turn will be our de-light 'Till by turn-ing, turn-ing we come round right.

73. HOLY SAVIOR CALL

An "extra song" ("sung in addition to the appointed songs") from the Alfred, Maine, community. c. 1847.

Lo, lo, saith the Sav - ior, my an - gels are sound-ing Their trum - pets to wak - en the sleep - ers a - round. There's no time for doubt-ing, there's no time for halt - ing, But stand to your post up - on God's ho - ly ground. Oh herk - en ye watchmen and strong men of Zi - on, Come up to the help of the Lord is the call, Oh shrink not in dan - ger but gird on your ar - mour And cleave to the stand-ards that you may not fall.

74. VERDANT GROVES
An "extra song" from Chosen Vale (Enfield, N. H.) c. 1847. Moderato.

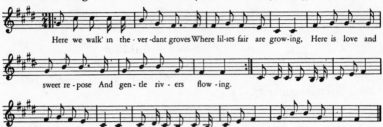

Here we walk' in the ver-dant groves Where lil-ies fair are grow-ing, Here is love and sweet re-pose And gen-tle riv-ers flow-ing.

75. I REJOICE IN THE CROSS
A Church order hymn from New Lebanon, 1849.

I re-joice in the cross of true self de-nial, Last-ing joys to my soul it doth bring, I am bound heav-en-ward and I'll bear ev'-ry trial That I meet on my way, and with tri-umph I'll sing. Oh pleas-ing thoughts, Oh hap-py re-flec-tions, I've no God I serve but the God of my pro-tec-tion, Yea! I'll wor-ship Him in plea-sure, in Him I do con-fide, I love His pu-ri-fy-ing work, with His way I'm sat-is-fied.

76. A SLOW SONG
Under the title, "A Slow Song," are many gravely intoned hymns of praise and reverence. The present example is not documented.

[138]

Thanks be un-to God, to our ho-ly Moth-er, To Je-sus the Sav-ior for this bless-ed gos-pel. Thanks be un-to God, to our ho-ly Moth-er, To Je-sus the Sav-ior for this bless-ed gos-pel. Oh I thank Mother Ann, our par-ents a-bove, Our lead-ers on earth and the an-gels of love.

77. BRAVE SOLDIER

A song sent from the Harvard society in the late 1840's to D. C. of New Lebanon. Mary Hazzard MS. The tune is probably derived from an older song: compare "Heaven's my Home" (No. 173 in "Spiritual Folk-Songs of Early America"). The latter, according to Dr. Jackson, is a re-make of a tune called 'Old Troy,' which "in turn is almost identical with, and probably made out of 'Wearing of the Green.'" "Brave Soldier" should proceed at a sprightly pace.

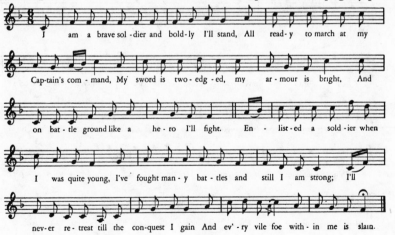

I am a brave sol-dier and bold-ly I'll stand, All read-y to march at my Cap-tain's com-mand, My sword is two-edg-ed, my ar-mour is bright, And on bat-tle ground like a he-ro I'll fight. En-list-ed a sold-ier when I was quite young, I've fought man-y bat-tles and still I am strong; I'll nev-er re-treat till the con-quest I gain And ev'-ry vile foe with-in me is slain.

78. THE SAVIOUR'S UNIVERSAL PRAYER

Originally composed for the meetings on Christmas, 1845, the Lord's Prayer was sung in many societies for many years, especially on the occasion of the mountain meetings. Usually it was followed by another hymn, "And again O Heavenly Father." These two spirituals are always found together in the manuscript, in this case the South Union (Ky.) hymnal of James Richardson. To be sung slowly and reverently.

Our Fa - ther who art in heaven, hal-low-ed be Thy name, Thy king-dom come,

Thy will be done, on earth as it is done in Heav-en. Give us this

day our dai - ly bread, And for-give us our debts as we for-give our debt -ors.

Leave us not in temp-ta - tion' but de - liv - er us from e - vil; For Thine is the

king - dom, the glo-ry and pow - er For ev - er - more. A - men.

And a-gain O heaven-ly Fath - er, Hear Thy chil-dren's hum-ble cry,

For o'er earth Thy wing doth hov-er, Bear-ing Judg-ments from on high.

While Thy jus - tice strews Thy Judg-ment, Lo! Thy mer -cy cries re - pent,

Help Thy chil -dren heed Thy warn-ings By the Proph - ets Thou hast sent.

79. A CUP OF REJOICING

Composed by Sallie Eades of South Union, Ky., Oct. 18, 1846, and transcribed Jan. 28, 1871 by M. Price. From Ja's H. Richardson's Hymn Book, South Union Shaker colony.

Like many of Sallie's songs, this one runs breathlessly and impatiently towards its conclusion. The Believers must have sung it with gay abandon, much as the Old Harp Singers of Nashville, Tenn. sing "Hosanna to Jesus," a southern spiritual which may itself have originated in a Kentucky Shaker settlement.

To conform to the notation and versification of the first stanza, the third line of each succeeding stanza is repeated once, followed by the first half of the fourth line; then the third line is sung twice, followed by the whole of the fourth line.

2. Pure love is the fountain and life is the stream
   Our spirits doth fill, our spirits doth fill,
   Here flowing, yea flowing all souls to redeem,
   For 'tis the Lord's will, for 'tis the Lord's will.

3. Sing praises sweet praises all ye of His flock,
   Let no one be still, let no one be still
   Whose feet he has placed on the permanent rock
   To do his pure will, to do his pure will.

4. We're moving, we're moving in this Jubilee,
   For who can be still, for who can be still,
   All bondage and death from our spirits shall flee,
   For 'tis the Lord's will, for 'tis the Lord's will.

5. We're sounding, resounding our trumpets of gold,
   The nations shall hear, the nations shall hear,
   Come gather, come gather ye into the fold,
   Salvation is near, salvation is near.

6. For the old accuser is surely cast out,
   The heavens doth ring, the heavens doth ring,
   The sons and the daughters of Zion doth shout
   In praise to their King, in praise to their King.

III

DANCES

THE ORIGINAL SHAKER DANCE was not an organized form of worship. Shaking or trembling, whirling, reeling, dancing, marching, running, stamping, shouting, gesticulating, falling to the ground—such exercises were in large part involuntary operations, precedents for which may be found in the history of many cults. Both the Quakers and French Prophets, from whom the Shakers stemmed, danced in the fullness of emotion. The subjects of the Kentucky Revival, who knew nothing of Shaker ritual until the Believers came into the west, were given to jerking, barking, marching and strange singing. The New Light Baptists of New England, a contemporary sect, were called "Merry Dancers." When the devotees of mystic or spiritual religions were wrought to an abnormal pitch of excitement, ecstasies found release in comparably extravagant forms of behavior.[1]

That the first meetings of the Manchester Shakers were formless and often chaotic is clear from the only account extant. "After assembling together and sitting a while in silent meditation," the record states, "they were taken with a mighty trembling . . . at other times they were affected . . . with a mighty shaking; and were occasionally exercised in singing, shouting, or walking the floor, under the influence of spiritual signs, shoving each other about,—or swiftly passing and repassing each other, like clouds agitated by a mighty wind.[2] In America the rituals were no less fantastic, presenting, according to the eyewitness Amos Taylor, "a perpetual scene of trembling, quivering, shaking, sighing, crying, groaning, screaming, jumping, singing, dancing and turning."

The singing meetings came first, "until they had got some footing, when it was immediately turned into heavy dancing, generally about forty or fifty men together and as many women separate by themselves in different rooms." "Heavy dancing" was performed

by a perpetual springing from the house floor, about four inches up and down, both in the men's and women's apartment, moving about as thick as they can crowd,

[1] See Davenport, F. M. Primitive Traits in Religious Revivals, esp. Chap. XI. New York, 1905.
[2] The Testimony of Christ's Second Appearing, p. xxv. Second Edition, Albany, 1810.

with extraordinary transport, singing sometimes one at a time, and sometimes more than one, making a perfect charm.

This elevation draws upon the nerves so as that they have intervals of shuddering as if they were in a strong fit of the ague.—They sometimes clap hands and leap so as to strike the joyce above their heads. They throw off their outside garments in these exercises, and spend their strength very cheerfully this way.[3]

"In the best part of their worship," Rathburn wrote of the first meetings at Niskeyuna,

everyone acts for himself, and almost every one different from the other; one will stand with his arms extended, acting over odd postures, which they call signs; another will be dancing, and sometimes hopping on one leg about the floor; another will fall to turning around, so swift, that if it be a woman, her clothes will be so filled with the wind, as though they were kept out by a hoop; another will be prostrate on the floor; another will be talking with somebody; and some sitting by, smoaking their pipes; some groaning most dismally; some trembling extremely; others acting as though all their nerves were convulsed; others swinging their arms, with all vigor, as though they were turning a wheel, etc. Then all break off, and have a spell of smoaking, and some times great fits of laughter. . . . They have several such exercises in a day, especially on the Sabbath.[4]

The earliest function of "labouring"—as the Shakers termed such exercises— was to shake off "doubts" and mortify the lusts of the flesh. Amidst all the spiritual gifts of the first meetings, comments the historian Youngs, "the pre- vailing motto and theme was *mortification, crucifixion of pride and self,* in

[3] Taylor, Amos. A Narrative of the Strange Principles, Conduct and Character Of the People known by the Name of Shakers, pp. 15-16. Worcester, 1782. Daniel Rathbun, in a pamphlet "Letter to James Whittacor" (Springfield, 1785), accused the Shakers of dancing naked. The charge was widely credited, though it apparently had no basis in fact—otherwise Taylor, Benjamin West, Col. James Smith, Marquis de Barbé-Marbois and other early critics of the sect would certainly have made use of it. Because Shaker labouring was a strenuous exercise, it was customary for the brethren to take off their coats, and for the sisters to dress lightly—habits which gave rise to exaggerated rumours.

One of these critics, William Plumer (op. cit.), noticed in 1782 that after a period of violent shak- ing several women embraced and saluted each other; two men then did the same, "a third clasped his arms around both, a fourth around them, and so on, until a dozen men were in that position, embrac- ing and saluting . . ." but he admitted that no man saluted or embraced a woman, nor any woman a man. For a long period quick dances sometimes ended in such "gifts." In 1827 a Shaker sister wrote in her journal: "we finished our meeting in hugging, in loving and blessing each other in sincerity and truth." And as late as 1870, in one of the wood-engravings of Boyd Houghton, sisters are seen kissing each other's cheeks while dancing.

[4] Rathbun, Valentine, op. cit.

spirit, which was sought for thro' mortification of the body."[5] Bowing, shaking, rolling on the floor, speaking with tongues, following the outstretched arm, testifying against the flesh "in all its branches," exposing sin, confessing faults— the tendency of all these gifts was "debasing" and "simplyfying." An early song called "The Zealous Laborers," two verses of which follow, reveals the underlying purpose of the original Shaker dance:

> O how I long to be released,
> From every feeling of the beast,
> No more to feel one poison dart,
> Of his vile stuff about my heart,
> But while I'm laboring with my might,
> This hateful beast will heave in sight,
> And every living step I tread
> I'll try to place it on his head.

> I need not think of gaining much,
> To give the floor an easy touch,
> Or labor in some handsome form,
> That scarce will keep my ancles warm,
> For I have not so far increased,
> That I can manage such a beast,
> Without my blood is nicely heat,
> And my whole body flows with sweat.

In "The Testimony of Christ's Second Appearing," the "bible" of the sect (1808), such "diverse operations" were called the "supernatural effects of the power of God." To worldly witnesses they might appear "unaccountable confusion . . . but such as were in the work, knew perfectly what those things meant, and felt, therein, the greatest possible order and harmony, it being to them the gift and work of God for the time then present." Since they were "frequently" led into the exercises of shaking and dancing, the Shakers were convinced that such was "acceptable work of God"—manifestations of a superhuman will to which they must automatically submit.[6]

Justification of dancing by appeal to the scriptures was a later development,

---

[5] Youngs MS.

[6] The authority for this last statement was Elder Calvin Green. (MS. dated 1861.) In 1843 the Shakers admitted to Charles Lane "that what was originally an involuntary emotion is now repeated as a voluntary duty." (C. L. "A Day with the Shakers." The Dial, Vol. IV, No. II, p. 168. October, 1843.)

a rationalization of practices which had aroused intense prejudices and open persecution. Early in the last century a dissenting member[7] was reminded that the exercise was "a worship among the ancient people of God." In a chapter on "the origin, practice and reasonableness of Dancing, as an act of Divine Worship," the authors of "A Summary View of the Millennial Church" (1823) alluded to the inspired psalmist who had sung, "let the children of Zion be joyful in their King, let them praise his name in the dance;" to Miriam the prophetess, who celebrated the deliverance of the children of Israel from Egyptian bondage "with timbrels and with dances;" to Jephthah's daughter, who welcomed her father with dances after his victory over the children of Ammon; to the form in which the victory of David and the Israelites over Goliath and the Philistine armies was celebrated; to the daughters of Shiloh who danced "in dances" at the yearly feast of the Lord; and when the ark of the covenant was established in Jerusalem, to the dances of David and all Israel before the Lord.[8] An undated Shaker broadside lists nineteen passages from the bible in favor of dancing, claiming that since not one passage speaks against it as sacred devotion, "all opposition to it, as Worship and Praise, is entirely unfounded upon Scripture."

The perversion and secularization of dancing by the wicked, Green and Wells argued, should not obliterate its divine function: "God has created man an active, intelligent being, possessing important powers and faculties, capable of serving himself according to his needs and circumstances; and he is required to devote these powers and faculties to the service of God." Every faculty, not the tongue alone, they maintained, should be devoted to the love and worship of the Creator: "Since we are blessed with hands and feet, those active and useful members of the body . . . shall we not acknowledge our obligations to God who gave them, by exercising them in our devotions to him? . . . The attitude of the body should be such as to express outwardly and assist the inward reverence of the soul." All should sing and dance in a true union of the spirit and in a uniform exercise—for "such must be the harmony of the christian church."[9]

[7] Brown, Thomas. An Account of the People called Shakers, p. 20. Troy, 1812. Brown was told that "dancing is the gift of God to the church, or the way in which it had been led. In this exercise we receive that strength, and consolation, to which the world are total strangers."

[8] A Summary View of the Millennial Church, etc., pp. 80-81, 84-85. (By Calvin Green and Seth Y. Wells.) Albany, 1823.

[9] No one was allowed to participate in the dance if he or she harbored any ill feeling. Among the Shakers' Millennial Laws (version of 1845) is the following statute:

"No member is allowed by the orders of God to present himself to worship Him when under

Like the songs and tunes, the nature of the dance changed as time went on. The earlier forms of labouring, in which each votary followed his or her own impulses, became known after 1785-86 as the "promiscuous," "quick" or "back" manner. These years saw the erection of a meeting-house at New Lebanon, the beginning of the communal organization of the society, and the introduction of a degree of order into the worship. Fanatical zeal had run its initial course, and the energies consumed in the long, frequent meetings—sometimes lasting until late at night—were slowly diverted into the arduous work of building up a "perfect" society. The success of such an enterprise, the leaders began to realize, rested in part on the good-will of those with whom the church must trade and to whom they must look for converts. They invited the world's people to their meetings, where their presence undoubtedly effected some modification and systematization of ritual.

The "square order shuffle"—the first distinct dance movement—was said to have been learned by Father Joseph Meacham, the American born organizer of the United Society, in a vision of angels dancing before the throne of God. The "shuffling manner," as described by Youngs, "consisted in taking three whole steps forward, turning, & taking three back, setting the foot straight forward at each end, & then going forward again three steps, and taking a double step, or 'tip tap,' as it is called, then receding three steps, with a 'tip tap;' this takes the turn part of the tune once; then it is repeated, in the same manner, then shuffle the set part once over."[10] A rhyme, recalled to this day by two aged sisters, aided the novices to attain a perfected technique:

> One, two, three, step,
> Foot straight at the turn.
> One, two, three, step,
> Equal length, solid tap.
> Take the shuffle, little back,
> Keep the body straight, erect,
> In every joint and bone.[11]

---

the condemnation of sin unconfessed. But all are required to present themselves to worship, with clean hands, pure hearts, and justified consciences." (MS.)

10 Youngs MS., op. cit.

11 With reference to the square or "holy order," the Millennial Laws directed Believers to take "three steps forward of an equal length, setting the feet straight forward at the turn . . . brethren should set off with the left foot, and sisters with the right; brethren turn to the right and sisters to the left." In the march all should start with the right foot. A variant of the above song is given on page 103.

From 1785 to 1788 the square order shuffle was the only organized dance. In the latter year Father Joseph introduced "the square step," a variant in which, at the "turn part" of the tune, the assembly advanced four times, taking three whole steps, and receded backwards three steps with *tip taps* at each end. The square step was usually performed at medium speed, but sometimes "very quick."

Labouring grew slower and slower during the last four or five years of Meacham's administration, and ceased altogether for two years after his death in 1796. The meetings became extremely "weighty" and solemn: no external gifts or operations enlivened the sense, and only the presiding elders spoke. But Mother Lucy Wright, who succeeded the puritanical Joseph as first in the central ministry, believed in animated worship—the angels *she* saw in vision were joyfully skipping around the celestial throne. Gradually the gifts and operations and signs returned, greatly accelerated in 1805 and 1806 by the ardours attending the Kentucky Revival. About that time the speed of the square order shuffle was increased to what was called "the skipping manner," and at times, for the benefit of the younger people, even the "back" or "promiscuous" manner was revived.[12] After 1807 the meetings at New Lebanon were held on Thursday and Saturday evenings and twice on the Sabbath.

With the advent of anthems, extra songs and written music, the service became more ritualistic and varied. In 1815, Mother Lucy taught the Shakers to motion with their arms and hands in exercise songs: in one form, to extend the forearms and hold the hands palms upward as if to receive spiritual blessings; in another, to suspend the hands and wave them inward as if gathering in spiritual good. Three years later another change occurred. The meetings had always begun with the two sexes facing each other in ranks—the elders in front, the oldest members next and the youngest in the rear—and singing a solemn song.[13] But in 1818 the ranks or files became more flexible. A group of

[12] Though few children were gathered into the order during the last decade of the eighteenth and opening years of the nineteenth century, more and more came in after 1805, the opening year of "the second gathering of the Church." This element enjoyed the experience of dancing, especially the freedom of "involuntary exercise." The traveler, T. Hamilton, noted that even in the organized dance "the more youthful and active introduced a few supererogatory gyrations, which were not attempted by the senior members; and one boy, in particular, signalized himself by a series of spirited saltations, not very dissimilar to the Highland fling." (Hamilton, T.: Men and Manners in America. Vol. II, p. 150. Philadelphia, 1833.)

[13] Before the early Shaker meetings began, a period of fifteen or twenty minutes called "retiring

singers formed a third rank or circle in the center or at the side of the room; and the ranks began certain "manouvers" which were later to develop into complex patterns. One of the initial steps in the evolution of the dance was made in the square step, which was varied so that the first ranks of both sexes faced the singers, the second faced the third, the fourth the fifth, and so on.

The first marches were introduced early in the year 1817—a simple pacing about the room, probably in single file to the tune of a "step song" or march. The "step march" was a lively movement, done in the so-called "step manner," forward-and-back or straight ahead, sometimes to form a circle.

The true "ring" dances, however, were not developed until 1822, soon after the death of Mother Lucy. In the earliest form the singers stood in the middle of the room, and the brethren and sisters (in separate files) placed themselves in a circle, advancing at the turn part of the tune and at the set part turning inward and dancing a single shuffle. Sometimes the round dances—the so-called "ring shuffle," for instance—were slow, but often they were "merry measures" done to a bounding elastic step, with hands "motioning" the time—"to quicken the spiritual elements and stir up zeal."

Other manners of worship were tried out in the period between 1822 and 1825. Individuals would turn while standing or marching in ranks; or the whole assembly would march in double file through the yards and orchards or along the highway, singing as they went. In a distinct movement, first seen in vision, the worshippers advanced in a four-square form, thus:

taking two steps from a to b, turning a quarter round, taking a double step, then two steps to c, then to d, and on to a in like manner, every fourth turn bringing the dancer back to the starting point.

In another form called "the hollow square" (first seen in vision at Harvard)

---

time" was spent in silent meditation—to prepare the spirit for worship. After 1800 the allotment was a half hour, when the signal to begin the meeting was given by rapping or ringing a bell. The custom of "retiring time" undoubtedly originated in the Quaker-influenced worship of the Manchester Shakers.

the sisters disposed themselves on one half of a square or rectangle and the brethren on the other, in the following manner:

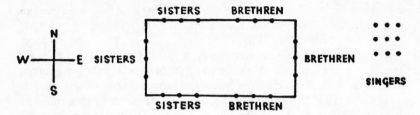

As Youngs explains the movement—done to a shuffling step—"the two ranks facing each other, on the north and south, advance up towards each other, turn round, and take three steps to the place of beginning, then advance up again and recede backward with the double step, the same as in square order shuffle: this takes half of the time once over, while the other two ranks on the east and west shuffle. In the other half (of the tune) the east and west ranks advance and recede while the others shuffle . . . There may be two squares in motion at the same time."[14]

A witness to a variant of the square order or hollow square shuffle thus explains the dance: "Dancing began by the members advancing, in a kind of marching step, for 6 paces, then 6 to the left, then 6 backwards, then 6 to the right. Thus they went on describing a square, in a jigging march, for a considerable time."[15] Music was furnished by three men who kept time by "pawing" with their hands "like dancing dogs" and chanting a wordless tune "in voices which might almost have been heard to the end of the valley."[16]

"Lively" dances, circular quick dances and even the "back" manner of worship became popular in the wake of a revival movement in 1827. Two variants of the ring dance were introduced in 1828. In one, called the "continuous ring" exercise, the brethren formed four ranks facing opposite ways, and the sisters likewise; then all "march(ed) forward in the song, turning from one rank into the other at the ends." Thus:

[14] Youngs MS., op. cit.

[15] The Penny Magazine of the Society for the Diffusion of Useful Knowledge. No. 361. November 18, 1837.

[16] Ibid.

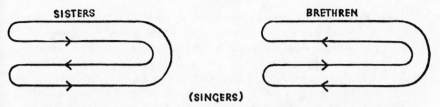

SISTERS   **BRETHREN**

(SINGERS)

In the other form brethren and sisters (always in separate files) placed themselves in two large circles, facing opposite ways and leaving a small opening or space on one side. The singers were stationed in the center of the circle. When the ranks moved forward they turned at the opening out of one circle into the other, bringing "every one to meet and see every one in the circles:"

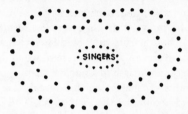

Known as the "endless chain" or "union dance," this was devised to promote union and make the worshippers conscious of an everlasting fellowship.[17]

[17] In a favorite "union dance" brethren and sisters lined up in two rows facing each other. The brother at one end stepped out and went down the brethren's line greeting each individual by grasping his hands and singing an appropriate song. A sister did the same along her line. Then all united in the refrain. Thus:

> *Brethren:* Take my hands in brotherly love
> In brotherly love, in brotherly love
> O, take my hands in brotherly love
> For love is our communion.
>
> *Sisters:* Take my hands in sisterly love
> In sisterly love, in sisterly love
> O take my hands in sisterly love
> For love is our communion.
>
> *All:* O I feel its good to be here
> Good to be here, good to be here,
> O I feel its good to be here
> Upon this present occasion.

Sometimes known as a "manual" song, this particular piece was probably sung to the "Mulberry Bush" tune of "Nancy Dawson."

There were several kinds of ring dances. A circle of singers might face inward in the center of the room, while around them moved two groups of dancers, two or three abreast, dancing in opposite directions to form "a wheel within a wheel." In its most elaborate pattern, developed later, four concentric circles of dancers were employed to symbolize the four dispensations or spiritual cycles of Shaker theology: the lion epoch, from Adam to Abraham; the calf epoch, from Abraham to Jesus; the face-of-a-man epoch, from Jesus to Mother Ann; and the flying-eagle epoch (the outer, greatest, all-inclusive circle), the period of the millennial church—Shakerism—"rising above the earthly order . . . into the pure and holy sphere of abstract Christianity." Walt Whitman, witnessing a "wheel" dance about 1853, was told that the singing in the center represented "the harmony and perfection to which all tend and there is God." [18]

The "sacred" marches also came to assume special significance—emblems of the travel of the soul heavenward. In their simplest forms they were solemn processions in single file, but the patterns would often change, brethren altering their file from three to two abreast and sisters from two to three, and vice versa; or all would march and countermarch in a single line.

Contemporary accounts of Shaker worship reveal how intricate and well-rehearsed the dance had become by the early 1830's. The following passage is from the "Subaltern's Furlough", by E. T. Coke, who visited a colony of Believers in 1832. Being a soldier, he was impressed by their skill in maneuvering, sense of tempo and well-drilled operations. The spectacle was like a theatrical performance, or better, a "field day," for

> there was such a scene of marching and counter-marching, slow step, quick step, and double quick step, advancing and retiring, forming open column and close column, perpendicular lines and oblique lines, that it was sufficient to puzzle and confound the clearest head of the lookers on.[19]

Henry Tudor, writing on July 14, 1831, after a visit to a New Lebanon meeting, called it "one of the most extraordinary scenes, and . . . one of the most marvellous exhibitions, that I have ever witnessed in any of the four quarters of the globe." After a short address a hymn was sung during which "they were

[18] Holloway, Emory. Walt Whitman's Visit to the Shakers. Colophon, Part 13, 1930.
[19] Coke, E. T. (Lt.) A Subaltern's Furlough, etc. Vol. I, p. 199. New York, 1833. Coke noted that the worshippers halted and sung in the slow parts of the air, then quickened their pace almost to a run at the livelier parts. Their hymns, however, were as monotonous as "an Indian chant at the feast of the Mohorum, or a Burman boat song as I have heard it on the Irawaddi, to which it bore no slight resemblance." (Ibid, p. 196.)

incessantly moving their feet; alternately raising each foot in a kind of dancing step, but without changing their position. This was accompanied by a grotesque inclination of their bodies from side to side." A short admonition followed, and another "monotonous air;" then all sat down.

In the dance proper, the men and women formed parallel lines with their backs to the spectators, and "commenced a sort of shuffling with their feet, and a motion with their hands in front of the breast, like the action of a dog in swimming." They advanced to the wall, retreated, then turned round and advanced and retreated in the opposite direction, marking time all the while with a song sung in an "unmusical, nasal tone."

Then the figure changed, the worshippers capering around the room in a double circle, "the females whirling round the inner ring, and the males describing the outward one." After reversing their positions in this movement, "they converted the two smaller circles into a single one, each sex following the other by alternate evolutions; and by a skilful manoeuvre, which I never saw executed but in the army, the men suddenly faced to the right about, slipped on one side, as to let the women pass, and met them at the opposite end of the room. . . . At certain intervals they came to a full stop, when they made salutations to each other (and) sang a verse or two." [20]

With the exception of movable benches, the meeting-rooms were bare of furniture, allowing ample space for the movements of a large assembly. Doors, window-frames and the rows of peg-boards along the wall were painted blue, the virgin color: sky blue in some cases, a green or Prussian-blue in others. Perhaps as a symbol of purity, the outside of the meeting-house, alone of all buildings in the community, was painted white. Blue and white were also the dominant colors in the Sabbathday dress. Though styles changed, early in the last century the prevalent costume of the brethren consisted of blue coats, blue and white pantaloons and black waistcoats; and of the sisters, long white gowns, blue petticoats, blue and white aprons, large neckerchiefs and white muslin or lawn caps.

During the time of the manifestations, 1837 to 1847, elaborations of the simple patterns were many: but such numbers as the winding march, lively line, lively ring, changeable dance, square check, double square, moving square, mother's star, cross and diamond, finished cross, Elder Benjamin's cross, square

---

[20] Tudor, Henry. Narrative of a Tour in North America, etc. Vol. I, p. 152, pp. 169-172. London, 1834.

and compass and mother's love—all stemmed from the fundamental operations. Marches also remained much alike, though given special titles such as "Sermon March," "Comforting March," "Pleasant March," "City of Peace March," "Purity March," "A Going March," "Sweet March to Heaven," "Little Children's March," "Sing Devotedly Order," "A Good Choice March" and a "Strawberry March"—the latter to be chanted as the sisters marched to and from the strawberry fields.

Aside from the strange rituals which characterized the decade of spiritualism, there were three new "dances." One known as the "checks" [21] was learned in 1837 from the entranced visionists. Another, introduced in 1840, was called "walking the Narrow Path"—"a slow, solemn kind of march in which one foot was placed right before the other." [22] The third exercise, first performed in 1847, was a sort of shuttling movement: ranks faced alternately north and south, passing each other as they marched. This is Youngs' diagram:

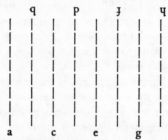

[21] "Dancing the checks" is nowhere described, but an aged Shaker sister has informed the writer that it was devised especially for the youth. She recalled one popular version in which groups of four young brethren or sisters stationed themselves, facing inward, in the form of a diamond. One pair of opposites would shuffle in their places while the other pair advanced, bowed solemnly as they met, and exchanged places; whereupon it was their turn to shuffle as the first pair stepped forward. The movement was animated, like the Virginia reel from which it may have stemmed, though it was performed with the utmost gravity.

[22] For this interestingly symbolic exercise the songs "Precept & Line" and "The Narrow Path" were composed:

> Precept on precept & line upon line
> We'll walk in the path our Mother has trod,
> Yea straight & clear straightness the pure way of God.
> (See p. 126)
> Day by day step by step
> In Mother's little narrow path we must go.
> And walk, yea walk exceeding low
>   to enter the kingdom of heaven

During those recurrent periods of emotional tension known as "awakenings" or "revivals", conscious control of ritual would often be lost in the cumulative excitement of worship. The earliest meetings in the history of each western community, for instance, duplicated those of the original assemblies at New Lebanon, Watervliet and the New England societies. Thus, at West Union, Indiana, worship began in 1815 with one or two solemn songs, but by then the singing was "entirely drounded by the Diferent Exercises:"

the Sound is like mighty thunderings, Some a Stamping with all their might and Roaring out against the nasty stinking beast. . . . Others turning with great Power and warring against the flesh, and at the same time a number Speaking with new tongues with Such Majestic Signs and motions that it makes the powers of Darkness tremble . . .[23]

Haskett tells of a "quick meeting" or "Shaker high" in the 1820's in which a solemn opening march was turned into quick or promiscuous dancing. When the elder exhorted the brethren and sisters "to labor for the gifts of Mother" and "shake off the flesh,"

a faint staggering seized the members, which, by degrees turned into a heavy shaking. Every position of which the human frame is susceptible, was to be seen. One leaping up, turning around; another flying around the room in the swift dance, and all engaged with their whole strength in every manner of action.[24]

When the elder finally called the meeting to order, all were greatly fatigued: "an awful silence ensued; the silence that must follow the most tremendous of wars, the war of body and soul."

On a Sabbath at Watervliet in 1838, Horace Greeley had a similar experience: "what was a measured dance" became a "wild, discordant frenzy." Gone were the gallopades, the double shuffles, the marches: "grave manhood and gentler girlhood" started "whirling round and round, two or three in company,

---

To show their humility the worshippers bowed low as they walked the "narrow way." The ritual suggests the attitude of the brethren and sisters at Ephrata as they passed through a low door to their hall of worship.

[23] Letter from Elder Archibald Meacham to the elders in the east. West Union Knox County Indiana Territory April 23, 1815. MS.

[24] Haskett, William J. Shakerism Unmasked, or The History of the Shakers, pp. 190-192. Pittsfield, 1828.

then each for him or herself."[25] Another example of what Youngs called the "back" manner of worship is related by the historian Gorrie:

As the singing and dancing progress (he writes), the Worshippers become more zealous, then frantic with excitement—until nothing but what the "World" would call disorder and confusion reigns. As the excitement increases, all order is forgotten, all unison of parts repudiated, each sings his own tune, each dances his own dance, or leaps, shouts, and exults with exceeding great joy—The more gifted of the Females engage in a kind of whirling motion, which they perform with seemingly incredible velocity their arms being extended horizontally and their dresses blown out like a Balloon all around their persons by the centrifugal force occasioned by the rapidity of their motion. After performing from Fifty to One thousand revolutions each, they either swoon away and fall into the arms of their Friends, or suddenly come to a stand, with apparently little or no dizziness produced. Sometimes the Worshippers engage in a race round the Room, with a sweeping motion of the Hands and Arms, intended to present the act of sweeping the Devil out of the Room.[26]

Some spectators, like Horace Greeley and George Combe, contemptuously likened the dancing postures of the Shakers to those of kangaroos, "penguins in procession" or dancing dogs; and popular opinion, reflected in the famous Imbert lithograph copied by Currier and others, conceived the worship as ridiculous or grotesque. Yet there were many who found the movements graceful and appropriate, and the worshippers themselves truly inspired. For Benson Lossing,[27] the artist-author, the scene was an "ethereal" one: the sisters clad in spotless white, with neat lawn caps, pure white kerchiefs over their bosoms, white handkerchiefs over their left arms, and shoes of a brilliant ultramarine blue prunella; the brethren in their pantaloons of blue linen, vests of a deeper blue and white cotton shirts. The earnestness and sincerity of Shaker worship, with its recognition "of the symbolical nature of all outward life," impressed another author, Ednah Littlehale,[28] more than that of our ordinary churches." And for the French Catholic writer, Mme. Therese Blanc, the dance was a thing of "sacred beauty:"

[25] Greeley, Horace. A Sabbath with the Shakers, p. 537. In The Knickerbocker, or New-York Monthly Magazine. Vol. XI. New York, 1838. See also Lamson, op. cit., pp. 86-88, and Fig. 20.

[26] Quoted from the Macdonald MS., op. cit. The passage is from Gorrie's "Churches and Sects in the United States" (1850).

[27] See unsigned article entitled "The Shakers," in Harpers' New Monthly Magazine, July, 1857, pp. 167-169. The sisters' handkerchiefs were spread on their laps during the intermissions between dances. The brethren always discarded their coats before "labouring."

[28] Mrs. Cheney, author of life of Louisa May Alcott, in a letter to Bronson Alcott dated July 19, 1849.

The movement of their hands—stretched forth to receive blessings or to offer to one's neighbor in prayer the grace he seeks—seems of very noble symbolism. And their feet barely touch earth in the rapid processional, accompanied by hymns to tunes sometimes very lively, at others remarkable for the repeated return (of) the same note, as in oriental music.[29]

As the Shaker order declined in numbers after the Civil War, it slowly lost that inner vitality of spirit which was the well-spring of its exuberant worship. The voice of the world grew more and more insistent, to the brethren especially, and Mother Ann's voice more distant. As the century advanced, the Shakers still sang of union, of holiness, of the joy of the virgin life. They still marched solemnly on their way to the heavenly Jerusalem. The preachers continued to argue the virtues of purity and a consecrate communal fellowship apart from the world. But worship was in the main a mechanical repetition of the old forms, revealing indeed the same saintly devotion to cause, but lacking the freshness of a movement renewed from within.[30] Rarely, in the latter quarter of the last century, occurred that "autointoxication of rapturous movement" of which Havelock Ellis speaks: "that self-forgetful union with the not-self which the mystic ever seeks." The dance became more sedate; the whirling and reeling ceased; the hymns, sung to the accompaniment of a harmonium or organ, failed to express that elusive quality which gave them Shaker significance. Though it may be many years yet before the last Believer leaves the last surviving community, the contributions of "the children of the free woman" to the religious folk art of America long ago came to a close.

[29] Bentzon, Th. (Mme. Therese Blanc) Choses et gens d' Amerique, pp. 86-87. Paris, 1898. (Translation through courtesy of Mr. John Alden, Springfield, Mass., Public library.) The description is of a meeting at the Alfred community in Maine. The author was told that the original dances of the Shakers resembled those of the dervishes.

[30] In his essay on "Goethe; or The Writer," Emerson used the Quakers and Shakers to illustrate his theme that rituals tend towards spiritless form: "The fiery reformer (he wrote) embodies his aspiration in some rite or covenant, and he and his friends cleave to the form and lose the aspiration. The Quaker has established Quakerism and the Shaker has established his monastery and his dance; and although each prates of spirit, there is no spirit, but repetition, which is anti-spiritual."

Writing of the period 1851-1856, Youngs lamented that "inspiration and notices from the spirit have been comparatively rare . . . Much depression of spirit has been felt, and struggling thro' dark & gloomy prospects, on account of apostacies, lifelessness & backslidings of unfaithful members, and the scanty ingathering from without. . . ."

IV

POST SCRIPT

ON ONLY TWO OCCASIONS, so far as we know, did Shaker dance and song find its way into the world. In 184-, a certain Mr. N. E. Chase, assisted by Miss L. A. Chase ("the miraculous Shaker tetotum") and a group of singers and dancers, performed for seven or more consecutive weeks to "overflowing houses" at the American Museum in New York. At "a grand levee" held on September 21, the following program [1] was rendered:

Part I

Song. O-le-er-lum-er-la. (A Shaker song learned by inspiration.)
Blanco. Holy Order and Square Order. (Dances)
Song. In the unknown tongue. (Learned by inspiration)
Le-Bala. Slow march and Quick March.

Part II

Song. Of the French Consul, sung and played on the spiritual Flute.
La-Bala. Square Hollow Company Labor. (A dance.)
Song. Osceola and Pocahontas.
La-Bala. Square Check Company Labor. (A dance.)

Part III

Song. The Reapers, with motions to mortify pride.
Song. Come Life, Shaker Life.
Blanco. Mother's Love, Company Labor. (A dance)

The Chases may have been apostates from the Canterbury society who knew the inspirational songs and dances of the sect and recognized their dramatic and commercial possibilities. Always an attraction to the curious, Shaker worship took such extraordinary forms during the manifestations that in 1842 the sabbath services were closed to the public. Large white wooden crosses—one inscribed with the words, "Enter not within these gates, for this is my Holy-Sanc-

---

[1] Taken from a broadside in possession of The New York Historical Society.

tuary saith the Lord. But pass ye by, and disturb not the peace of the quiet, upon my Holy Sabbath"—kept visitors away until the meetings were re-opened in 1845. It may well be that the Chases decided to exploit Shaker spiritualism during this period.

"Even Horn," a member of Fellows Minstrels, also saw in the Shaker dance-song and racial impersonations an opportunity for stage entertainment. In 1851, Horn composed "Fi, Hi, Hi The Black Shakers," [2] a song and polka originally performed by Fellows Ethiopian Troupe. The words follow:

> Bress dat lub-ly yal-lar gal,
> De white folks call miss Dinah;
> Oh! pi-ty me ye shakers all
> And tell me where I'll find her,
> She's gone a-way to Leb'non state
> To hoe de corn and bake de cake;
> Massa says, it is to late:
> Let her go to Leb'non state.

> Fi hi hi lum i dum didle lum
> Fi hi hi ri tidle lum i dum
> Fi hi hi.

> And since she's gone and left me,
> I dont know what I'll do;
> I'll buy a rope and drown myself:
> Dat make her mad I know.
> She's gone away to Leb'non state
> To hoe de corn and bake de cake;
> And Massa says, it is to late:
> Let her go to Leb'non state.

> Fi hi hi lum i dum didle lum
> Fi hi hi ri tidle lum i dum
> Fi hi hi.

[2] Published by Firth, Pond & Co. 1 Franklin Square, New York; F. D. Benteen, Baltimore, Md.; and Lee & Walker, Philadelphia.

SELECTED REFERENCES

ANDREWS, EDWARD D. Shaker Songs. (In) The Musical Quarterly, Vol. XXIII, No. 4. October, 1937. *New York.*

BENTZON, TH. (Mme. Therese Blanc) Choses et gens d'Amerique. *Paris, 1898.*

BLINN, HENRY C. The Manifestation of Spiritualism among the Shakers, 1837-1847. *East Canterbury, N. H., 1899.*

BROWN, THOMAS. An Account of the People called Shakers: their faith, doctrines, and practice, exemplified in the life, conversations, and experience of the author during the time he belonged to the society. To which is affixed a history of their rise and progress to the present day. *Troy, 1812.*

BUCKINGHAM, J. S. America, Historical, Statistic, and Descriptive. In two volumes. *New York, 1841.*

COKE, E. T. (Lt.). A Subaltern's Furlough: Descriptive of Scenes in Various Parts of the United States, Upper and Lower Canada, New-Brunswick, and Nova Scotia, during the summer and autumn of 1832. In two volumes. *New York, 1833.*

Collection of anthems revealed by the spirits, 1837-1848. (James Holmes, comp.) *West Gloucester, Me., n. d.*

Collection (A) of Harmonies and Melodies, adapted to sacred worship. *Canterbury, 1878.*

Collection (A) of Hymns and Anthems adapted to public worship. *East Canterbury, N. H., 1892.*

Collections on the History of Albany. (Joel Munsell, ed.) *Albany, 1867.*

DAVENPORT, FREDERICK MORGAN. Primitive Traits in Religious Revivals. *New York, 1905.*

DYER, MARY. A portraiture of Shakerism, exhibiting a general view of their character and conduct, from the first appearance of Ann Lee in New England, down to the present time. *Concord (N. H.), 1822.*

ELKINS, HERVEY. Fifteen years in the senior order of Shakers: a narrative of facts concerning that singular people. *Hanover (N. H.), 1853.*

Extract from an unpublished manuscript on Shaker history, giving an accurate description of their songs, dances, marches, visions, visits to the spirit land, etc. By an eye-witness. *Boston, 1850.*

GREELEY, HORACE. A Sabbath with the Shakers. (In) The Knickerbocker, or New-York Monthly Magazine, Vol. XI. *New York, 1838.*

HAMILTON, T. Men and Manners in America. In two volumes. Second American edition. *Philadelphia, 1833.*

HASKELL, RUSSEL. A musical expositor: or, a treatise on the rules and elements of music; adapted to the most approved method of musical writing. *New York, 1847.*

HASKETT, WILLIAM J. Shakerism Unmasked, or the History of the Shakers; including a form politic of their government as Councils, Orders, Gifts, with an exposition of The Five Orders of Shakerism, and Ann Lee's grand foundation vision, in sealed pages. With some extracts from their private hymns which have never appeared before the public. *Pittsfield, 1828.*

HINDS, WILLIAM ALFRED. American Communities. *Oneida, N. Y., 1878.*

HOLLOWAY, EMORY. Walt Whitman's Visit to the Shakers. With Whitman's notebook containing his description & observations of the Shaker group at Mt. Lebanon. (In) The Colophon, First Issue, Spring, 1930. Part Thirteen. *New York, 1933.*

HOWELLS, WILLIAM DEAN. Three Villages. *Boston, 1884.*

JACKSON, GEORGE PULLEN. Spiritual Folk-Songs of Early America. *New York, 1937.*

LAMSON, DAVID R. Two Years' experience among the Shakers: being a description of the manners and customs of that people, the nature and policy of their government, their marvellous intercourse with the spiritual world, the object and uses of confession, their inquisition, in short, a condensed view of Shakerism as it is. *West Boylston (Mass.), 1848.*

MacLEAN, J. P. Shakers of Ohio. *Columbus, Ohio, 1907.*

MAXWELL, COL. A. M., K. H. A Run through the United States, during the autumn of 1840. In two volumes. *London, 1841.*

McNEMAR, RICHARD. The Kentucky revival; or, a short history of the late extraordinary outpouring of the spirit of God in the western states of America, agreeably to scripture promises and prophecies concerning the latter day: with a brief account of the entrance and progress of what the world call Shakerism among the subjects of the late revival in Ohio and Kentucky . . . *Cincinnati, 1807. (Reprinted in Albany, 1808.)*

Millennial Praises, Containing a Collection of Gospel Hymns, in Four Parts; Adapted to the Day of Christ's Second Appearing. Composed for the use of his people. *Hancock (Mass.), 1813.*

Musical Messenger, The. A Compilation of Hymns, Slow and Quick Marches, etc., used in worship by Believers. Published by The United Society of Believers, Union Village, Ohio. F. Estes. *Lebanon, Ohio. (n. d.)* (This and The Sacred Repository (Canterbury, 1852) are the only printed books to contain letter notes. In the Union Village hymnal the length of the notes are designated by the *kind* of type employed—italics, old English, etc.)

NORDHOFF, CHARLES. The Communistic Societies of the United States. *New York, 1875.*

Original (The) Shaker Communities in New England. (The Plumer Papers. Frank Sanborn, ed.) (In) The New England Magazine, New Series, Vol. 22. *1900.*

Original Shaker Music. (Published by the North Family, Mount Lebanon, N. Y.) *New York, 1893.*

Penny Magazine (The) of the Society for the Diffusion of Useful Knowledge. No. 361. *November 18, 1837.*

RATHBUN, VALENTINE. Some Brief Hints, of a Religious Scheme, Taught and Propagated by a Number of Europeans, living in a Place called Nisqueunia, in the State of New-York. *Norwich (Conn.), 1781.*

Repository (A) of Music, containing elementary and advanced lessons, selected from the works of able teachers. *Canterbury, N. H. 1880.*

Return (A) of departed spirits of the highest characters of distinction, as well as the indiscriminate of all nations, into the bodies of the "Shakers," or "United Society of Believers" in the second advent of the Messiah. By an associate of the Society. *Philadelphia, 1843.*

Revelation (A) of the Extraordinary Visitation of Departed Spirits of Distinguished Men and Women of all nations, and their Manifestations Through the Living Bodies of the "Shakers." By a guest of the "community" near Watervliet, N. Y. *Philadelphia, 1869.*

Sacred Repository (A) of Anthems and Hymns, for devotional worship and praise. *Canterbury, N. H. 1852.*

SEARS, CLARA ENDICOTT. Gleanings from Old Shaker Journals. *Boston, 1916.*

Selection of devotional melodies. *Canterbury, N. H. 1876.*

Selection (A) of Hymns and Poems; for the Use of Believers. By Philos Harmoniae (Richard McNemar). *Watervliet, Ohio, 1833.*

Shaker Anthems and Hymns, arranged for divine worship. *Shaker Village, N. H. 1883.*

Shaker Hymnal. By the Canterbury Shakers. *Boston, 1908.*

Shaker Music. *East Canterbury, N. H., 1875-1892.* (Printed "at different periods of time.")

Shaker music. Inspirational hymns and melodies illustrative of the resurrection life and testimony of the Shakers. *Albany, 1875.* (A revised edition appeared in 1884 with a New York imprint.)

Shaker Songs and Music. By P. B. (Phillips Barry) and Mellinger E. Henry. (In) Bulletin of the Folk-Song Society of the Northeast, No. 4. *Cambridge, 1932.*

Shakers Dance. New American Dance for Piano. Music by George Denis, Op. 99. Dedicated to Miss Margaret Wilson, U. S. A. (n.d.) On the cover is a crude lithograph entitled "Les Shakers de Lebanon executant leur danse (d' après une lithographie de Mr Alophe. Bibliothèque Nat^{le} de Paris)." American publisher, M. Witmark & Sons, N. Y. Denis' "theorie" contemplated a dance by couples!

Shakers, The. (By Benson J. Lossing.) In Harper's New Monthly Magazine, No. LXXXVI. *July, 1857.*

Summary (A) View of the Millennial Church, or United Society of Believers (commonly called Shakers). Comprising the rise, progress and practical order of the society; together with the general principles of their faith and testimony. (By Calvin Green and Seth Y. Wells.) *Albany, 1823.*

TAYLOR, AMOS. A Narrative of the Strange Principles, Conduct and Character of the People known by the Name of Shakers. *Worcester, 1782.*

Testimonies of the life, character, revelations and doctrines of our ever blessed mother Ann Lee, and the elders with her; through whom the word of eternal life was opened in this day of Christ's second appearing. (Rufus Bishop, comp. Revised by Seth Y. Wells.) *Hancock, 1816.*

Testimony (The) of Christ's Second Appearing, Containing a general statement of all things pertaining to the faith and practice of the church of God in this latter-day. (By Benjamin S. Youngs, David Darrow and John Meacham.) *Lebanon, State of Ohio, 1808.*

TUDOR, HENRY. Narrative of a Tour in North America. In two volumes. *London, 1834.* (Letter VII.)

VIGNE, GODFREY T. Six Months in America. *Philadelphia, 1833.*

WAKEFIELD, PRISCILLA. Excursions in North America. *London, 1806.*

WHITE, ANNA and TAYLOR, LEILA. Shakerism: its Meaning and Message. Embracing an Historical Account, Statement of Belief and Spiritual Experience of the Church from its Rise to the Present Day. *Columbus (Ohio), 1905.*

YOUNGS, ISAAC N. A Short Abridgement Of the Rules of Music. With Lessons For Exercise, and A few Observations; For new Beginners. *Printed at New Lebanon; 1843.* (Reprinted 1846.)

Manuscripts

Account (An) of the Meetings Held in the City of Peace, City of Union, and City of Love, On the 25th of Dec. 1845.

A list of Different Tribes of Indians & From the world of Spirits Who came to learn the way of God, of Mother's children on Earth. South Hous. *Wisdom's Valley (Watervliet), Oct. 26, 1842.*

BUSHNELL, SALLY. A Spiritual Journal Commenced June 1st, 1841. *Canaan (N.Y.) Lower Family.*

Eye-witness account of a mountain meeting of the New Lebanon Shakers in 1843. (Anon.) *New Lebanon Springs, May 21, 1843.*

Inspirational messages, or sacred communications to the Shaker instruments. (Collection dating from 1840 to 1845.)

Little (A) Book Containing a Short Word from Holy Mother Wisdom, Concerning the Robes & Dresses That Are Prepared for All Such As Go Up to the Feast of the Lord, or Attend to Her Holy Passover. *Copied July 20, 1842. Hancock.*

MACDONALD, A. J. The Macdonald Manuscript. (The original notes of the itinerant Scotch printer and student of American socialisms are in the Yale University library. Portions of the MS. were used by John Humphrey Noyes in his "History of American Socialisms," Philadelphia, 1870.)

Manuscript hymnals. Hymns, anthems, spiritual songs, gift songs, extra songs, marches, labouring tunes, etc. (Collections dating from 1808 to 1858.)

Millennial Laws, or Gospel Statutes and Ordinances adapted to the Day of Christ's Second Appearing.

Selected References

Given and established in the Church for the protection thereof by Father Joseph Meacham and Mother Lucy Wright, The presiding Ministry, and by their Successors The Ministry and Elders. Recorded at New Lebanon Augst 17th, 1821. Revised and re-established by the Ministry and Elders Octr 1845.

Record (A) Kept of the Several Meetings held upon Mount Sinai by the Family Orders on Days of the Feasts. *Hancock, 1842-1845.*

Records of meetings. (Collection.)

STEWART, PHILEMON. A General Statement of the Holy Laws of Zion. *New Lebanon, 1840.*

YOUNGS, ISAAC N. A Concise View Of the Church of God and of Christ, On Earth, Having its foundation In the faith of Christ's first and Second Appearing. *New Lebanon 1856.*

YOUNGS, ISAAC N. and BUCKINGHAM, D. A. A Treatise on Music; agreeably to the Plan established and adopted at New Lebanon and Watervliet, N. Y. *1840.*

Index of First Lines of Songs*

*Numbers in parentheses (italics) refer to songs with melodic accompaniment. Other numbers are page references.

Index of Tunes and Songs with Melodic Accompaniment*

*Numbers in parentheses (italics) refer to the song or tune numbers in "A Collection of Tunes with Texts."

A CATALOG OF
SELECTED DOVER BOOKS
IN ALL FIELDS OF INTEREST

A CATALOG OF SELECTED DOVER BOOKS IN ALL FIELDS OF INTEREST

CONCERNING THE SPIRITUAL IN ART, Wassily Kandinsky. Pioneering work by father of abstract art. Thoughts on color theory, nature of art. Analysis of earlier masters. 12 illustrations. 80pp. of text. 5⅜ × 8½. 23411-8 Pa. $2.50

LEONARDO ON THE HUMAN BODY, Leonardo da Vinci. More than 1200 of Leonardo's anatomical drawings on 215 plates. Leonardo's text, which accompanies the drawings, has been translated into English. 506pp. 8⅜ × 11¾. 24483-0 Pa. $10.95

GOBLIN MARKET, Christina Rossetti. Best-known work by poet comparable to Emily Dickinson, Alfred Tennyson. With 46 delightfully grotesque illustrations by Laurence Housman. 64pp. 4 × 6¾. 24516-0 Pa. $2.50

THE HEART OF THOREAU'S JOURNALS, edited by Odell Shepard. Selections from *Journal*, ranging over full gamut of interests. 228pp. 5⅜ × 8½. 20741-2 Pa. $4.50

MR. LINCOLN'S CAMERA MAN: MATHEW B. BRADY, Roy Meredith. Over 300 Brady photos reproduced directly from original negatives, photos. Lively commentary. 368pp. 8⅜ × 11¼. 23021-X Pa. $11.95

PHOTOGRAPHIC VIEWS OF SHERMAN'S CAMPAIGN, George N. Barnard. Reprint of landmark 1866 volume with 61 plates: battlefield of New Hope Church, the Etawah Bridge, the capture of Atlanta, etc. 80pp. 9 × 12. 23445-2 Pa. $6.00

A SHORT HISTORY OF ANATOMY AND PHYSIOLOGY FROM THE GREEKS TO HARVEY, Dr. Charles Singer. Thoroughly engrossing non-technical survey. 270 illustrations. 211pp. 5⅜ × 8½. 20389-1 Pa. $4.50

REDOUTE ROSES IRON-ON TRANSFER PATTERNS, Barbara Christopher. Redouté was botanical painter to the Empress Josephine; transfer his famous roses onto fabric with these 24 transfer patterns. 80pp. 8¼ × 10⅞. 24292-7 Pa. $3.50

THE FIVE BOOKS OF ARCHITECTURE, Sebastiano Serlio. Architectural milestone, first (1611) English translation of Renaissance classic. Unabridged reproduction of original edition includes over 300 woodcut illustrations. 416pp. 9⅜ × 12¼. 24349-4 Pa. $14.95

CARLSON'S GUIDE TO LANDSCAPE PAINTING, John F. Carlson. Authoritative, comprehensive guide covers, every aspect of landscape painting. 34 reproductions of paintings by author; 58 explanatory diagrams. 144pp. 8⅜ × 11. 22927-0 Pa. $4.95

101 PUZZLES IN THOUGHT AND LOGIC, C.R. Wylie, Jr. Solve murders, robberies, see which fishermen are liars—purely by reasoning! 107pp. 5⅜ × 8½. 20367-0 Pa. $2.00

TEST YOUR LOGIC, George J. Summers. 50 more truly new puzzles with new turns of thought, new subtleties of inference. 100pp. 5⅜ × 8½. 22877-0 Pa. $2.25

THE MURDER BOOK OF J.G. REEDER, Edgar Wallace. Eight suspenseful stories by bestselling mystery writer of 20s and 30s. Features the donnish Mr. J.G. Reeder of Public Prosecutor's Office. 128pp. 5⅜ × 8½. (Available in U.S. only)
24374-5 Pa. $3.50

ANNE ORR'S CHARTED DESIGNS, Anne Orr. Best designs by premier needlework designer, all on charts: flowers, borders, birds, children, alphabets, etc. Over 100 charts, 10 in color. Total of 40pp. 8¼ × 11. 23704-4 Pa. $2.25

BASIC CONSTRUCTION TECHNIQUES FOR HOUSES AND SMALL BUILDINGS SIMPLY EXPLAINED, U.S. Bureau of Naval Personnel. Grading, masonry, woodworking, floor and wall framing, roof framing, plastering, tile setting, much more. Over 675 illustrations. 568pp. 6½ × 9¼. 20242-9 Pa. $8.95

MATISSE LINE DRAWINGS AND PRINTS, Henri Matisse. Representative collection of female nudes, faces, still lifes, experimental works, etc., from 1898 to 1948. 50 illustrations. 48pp. 8⅜ × 11¼. 23877-6 Pa. $2.50

HOW TO PLAY THE CHESS OPENINGS, Eugene Znosko-Borovsky. Clear, profound examinations of just what each opening is intended to do and how opponent can counter. Many sample games. 147pp. 5⅜ × 8½. 22795-2 Pa. $2.95

DUPLICATE BRIDGE, Alfred Sheinwold. Clear, thorough, easily followed account: rules, etiquette, scoring, strategy, bidding; Goren's point-count system, Blackwood and Gerber conventions, etc. 158pp. 5⅜ × 8½. 22741-3 Pa. $3.00

SARGENT PORTRAIT DRAWINGS, J.S. Sargent. Collection of 42 portraits reveals technical skill and intuitive eye of noted American portrait painter, John Singer Sargent. 48pp. 8¼ × 11⅛. 24524-1 Pa. $2.95

ENTERTAINING SCIENCE EXPERIMENTS WITH EVERYDAY OBJECTS, Martin Gardner. Over 100 experiments for youngsters. Will amuse, astonish, teach, and entertain. Over 100 illustrations. 127pp. 5⅜ × 8½. 24201-3 Pa. $2.50

TEDDY BEAR PAPER DOLLS IN FULL COLOR: A Family of Four Bears and Their Costumes, Crystal Collins. A family of four Teddy Bear paper dolls and nearly 60 cut-out costumes. Full color, printed one side only. 32pp. 9¼ × 12¼.
24550-0 Pa. $3.50

NEW CALLIGRAPHIC ORNAMENTS AND FLOURISHES, Arthur Baker. Unusual, multi-useable material: arrows, pointing hands, brackets and frames, ovals, swirls, birds, etc. Nearly 700 illustrations. 80pp. 8⅜ × 11¼.
24095-9 Pa. $3.75

DINOSAUR DIORAMAS TO CUT & ASSEMBLE, M. Kalmenoff. Two complete three-dimensional scenes in full color, with 31 cut-out animals and plants. Excellent educational toy for youngsters. Instructions; 2 assembly diagrams. 32pp. 9¼ × 12¼. 24541-1 Pa. $3.95

SILHOUETTES: A PICTORIAL ARCHIVE OF VARIED ILLUSTRATIONS, edited by Carol Belanger Grafton. Over 600 silhouettes from the 18th to 20th centuries. Profiles and full figures of men, women, children, birds, animals, groups and scenes, nature, ships, an alphabet. 144pp. 8⅜ × 11¼. 23781-8 Pa. $4.95

25 KITES THAT FLY, Leslie Hunt. Full, easy-to-follow instructions for kites made from inexpensive materials. Many novelties. 70 illustrations. 110pp. 5⅜ × 8½. 22550-X Pa. $2.25

PIANO TUNING, J. Cree Fischer. Clearest, best book for beginner, amateur. Simple repairs, raising dropped notes, tuning by easy method of flattened fifths. No previous skills needed. 4 illustrations. 201pp. 5⅜ × 8½. 23267-0 Pa. $3.50

EARLY AMERICAN IRON-ON TRANSFER PATTERNS, edited by Rita Weiss. 75 designs, borders, alphabets, from traditional American sources. 48pp. 8¼ × 11. 23162-3 Pa. $1.95

CROCHETING EDGINGS, edited by Rita Weiss. Over 100 of the best designs for these lovely trims for a host of household items. Complete instructions, illustrations. 48pp. 8¼ × 11. 24031-2 Pa. $2.25

FINGER PLAYS FOR NURSERY AND KINDERGARTEN, Emilie Poulsson. 18 finger plays with music (voice and piano); entertaining, instructive. Counting, nature lore, etc. Victorian classic. 53 illustrations. 80pp. 6½ × 9¼. 22588-7 Pa. $1.95

BOSTON THEN AND NOW, Peter Vanderwarker. Here in 59 side-by-side views are photographic documentations of the city's past and present. 119 photographs. Full captions. 122pp. 8¼ × 11. 24312-5 Pa. $6.95

CROCHETING BEDSPREADS, edited by Rita Weiss. 22 patterns, originally published in three instruction books 1939-41. 39 photos, 8 charts. Instructions. 48pp. 8¼ × 11. 23610-2 Pa. $2.00

HAWTHORNE ON PAINTING, Charles W. Hawthorne. Collected from notes taken by students at famous Cape Cod School; hundreds of direct, personal *apercus*, ideas, suggestions. 91pp. 5⅜ × 8½. 20653-X Pa. $2.50

THERMODYNAMICS, Enrico Fermi. A classic of modern science. Clear, organized treatment of systems, first and second laws, entropy, thermodynamic potentials, etc. Calculus required. 160pp. 5⅜ × 8½. 60361-X Pa. $4.00

TEN BOOKS ON ARCHITECTURE, Vitruvius. The most important book ever written on architecture. Early Roman aesthetics, technology, classical orders, site selection, all other aspects. Morgan translation. 331pp. 5⅜ × 8½. 20645-9 Pa. $5.50

THE CORNELL BREAD BOOK, Clive M. McCay and Jeanette B. McCay. Famed high-protein recipe incorporated into breads, rolls, buns, coffee cakes, pizza, pie crusts, more. Nearly 50 illustrations. 48pp. 8¼ × 11. 23995-0 Pa. $2.00

THE CRAFTSMAN'S HANDBOOK, Cennino Cennini. 15th-century handbook, school of Giotto, explains applying gold, silver leaf; gesso; fresco painting, grinding pigments, etc. 142pp. 6⅛ × 9¼. 20054-X Pa. $3.50

FRANK LLOYD WRIGHT'S FALLINGWATER, Donald Hoffmann. Full story of Wright's masterwork at Bear Run, Pa. 100 photographs of site, construction, and details of completed structure. 112pp. 9¼ × 10. 23671-4 Pa. $6.50

OVAL STAINED GLASS PATTERN BOOK, C. Eaton. 60 new designs framed in shape of an oval. Greater complexity, challenge with sinuous cats, birds, mandalas framed in antique shape. 64pp. 8¼ × 11. 24519-5 Pa. $3.50

THE BOOK OF WOOD CARVING, Charles Marshall Sayers. Still finest book for beginning student. Fundamentals, technique; gives 34 designs, over 34 projects for panels, bookends, mirrors, etc. 33 photos. 118pp. 7¾ × 10⅝. 23654-4 Pa. $3.95

CARVING COUNTRY CHARACTERS, Bill Higginbotham. Expert advice for beginning, advanced carvers on materials, techniques for creating 18 projects— mirthful panorama of American characters. 105 illustrations. 80pp. 8⅜ × 11. 24135-1 Pa. $2.50

300 ART NOUVEAU DESIGNS AND MOTIFS IN FULL COLOR, C.B. Grafton. 44 full-page plates display swirling lines and muted colors typical of Art Nouveau. Borders, frames, panels, cartouches, dingbats, etc. 48pp. 9⅜ × 12¼. 24354-0 Pa. $6.00

SELF-WORKING CARD TRICKS, Karl Fulves. Editor of *Pallbearer* offers 72 tricks that work automatically through nature of card deck. No sleight of hand needed. Often spectacular. 42 illustrations. 113pp. 5⅜ × 8½. 23334-0 Pa. $3.50

CUT AND ASSEMBLE A WESTERN FRONTIER TOWN, Edmund V. Gillon, Jr. Ten authentic full-color buildings on heavy cardboard stock in H-O scale. Sheriff's Office and Jail, Saloon, Wells Fargo, Opera House, others. 48pp. 9¼ × 12¼. 23736-2 Pa. $3.95

CUT AND ASSEMBLE AN EARLY NEW ENGLAND VILLAGE, Edmund V. Gillon, Jr. Printed in full color on heavy cardboard stock. 12 authentic buildings in H-O scale: Adams home in Quincy, Mass., Oliver Wight house in Sturbridge, smithy, store, church, others. 48pp. 9¼ × 12¼. 23536-X Pa. $3.95

THE TALE OF TWO BAD MICE, Beatrix Potter. Tom Thumb and Hunca Munca squeeze out of their hole and go exploring. 27 full-color Potter illustrations. 59pp. 4¼ × 5½. (Available in U.S. only) 23065-1 Pa. $1.50

CARVING FIGURE CARICATURES IN THE OZARK STYLE, Harold L. Enlow. Instructions and illustrations for ten delightful projects, plus general carving instructions. 22 drawings and 47 photographs altogether. 39pp. 8⅜ × 11. 23151-8 Pa. $2.50

A TREASURY OF FLOWER DESIGNS FOR ARTISTS, EMBROIDERERS AND CRAFTSMEN, Susan Gaber. 100 garden favorites lushly rendered by artist for artists, craftsmen, needleworkers. Many form frames, borders. 80pp. 8¼ × 11. 24096-7 Pa. $3.50

CUT & ASSEMBLE A TOY THEATER/THE NUTCRACKER BALLET, Tom Tierney. Model of a complete, full-color production of Tchaikovsky's classic. 6 backdrops, dozens of characters, familiar dance sequences. 32pp. 9⅜ × 12¼. 24194-7 Pa. $4.50

ANIMALS: 1,419 COPYRIGHT-FREE ILLUSTRATIONS OF MAMMALS, BIRDS, FISH, INSECTS, ETC., edited by Jim Harter. Clear wood engravings present, in extremely lifelike poses, over 1,000 species of animals. 284pp. 9 × 12. 23766-4 Pa. $9.95

MORE HAND SHADOWS, Henry Bursill. For those at their 'finger ends," 16 more effects—Shakespeare, a hare, a squirrel, Mr. Punch, and twelve more—each explained by a full-page illustration. Considerable period charm. 30pp. 6½ × 9¼. 21384-6 Pa. $1.95

SURREAL STICKERS AND UNREAL STAMPS, William Rowe. 224 haunting, hilarious stamps on gummed, perforated stock, with images of elephants, geisha girls, George Washington, etc. 16pp. one side. 8¼ × 11.   24371-0 Pa. $3.50

GOURMET KITCHEN LABELS, Ed Sibbett, Jr. 112 full-color labels (4 copies each of 28 designs). Fruit, bread, other culinary motifs. Gummed and perforated. 16pp. 8¼ × 11.   24087-8 Pa. $2.95

PATTERNS AND INSTRUCTIONS FOR CARVING AUTHENTIC BIRDS, H.D. Green. Detailed instructions, 27 diagrams, 85 photographs for carving 15 species of birds so life-like, they'll seem ready to fly! 8¼ × 11.   24222-6 Pa. $2.75

FLATLAND, E.A. Abbott. Science-fiction classic explores life of 2-D being in 3-D world. 16 illustrations. 103pp. 5⅜ × 8.   20001-9 Pa. $2.00

DRIED FLOWERS, Sarah Whitlock and Martha Rankin. Concise, clear, practical guide to dehydration, glycerinizing, pressing plant material, and more. Covers use of silica gel. 12 drawings. 32pp. 5⅜ × 8½.   21802-3 Pa. $1.00

EASY-TO-MAKE CANDLES, Gary V. Guy. Learn how easy it is to make all kinds of decorative candles. Step-by-step instructions. 82 illustrations. 48pp. 8¼ × 11.
     23881-4 Pa. $2.50

SUPER STICKERS FOR KIDS, Carolyn Bracken. 128 gummed and perforated full-color stickers: GIRL WANTED, KEEP OUT, BORED OF EDUCATION, X-RATED, COMBAT ZONE, many others. 16pp. 8¼ × 11.   24092-4 Pa. $2.50

CUT AND COLOR PAPER MASKS, Michael Grater. Clowns, animals, funny faces...simply color them in, cut them out, and put them together, and you have 9 paper masks to play with and enjoy. 32pp. 8¼ × 11.   23171-2 Pa. $2.25

A CHRISTMAS CAROL: THE ORIGINAL MANUSCRIPT, Charles Dickens. Clear facsimile of Dickens manuscript, on facing pages with final printed text. 8 illustrations by John Leech, 4 in color on covers. 144pp. 8⅜ × 11¼.
     20980-6 Pa. $5.95

CARVING SHOREBIRDS, Harry V. Shourds & Anthony Hillman. 16 full-size patterns (all double-page spreads) for 19 North American shorebirds with step-by-step instructions. 72pp. 9¼ × 12¼.   24287-0 Pa. $4.95

THE GENTLE ART OF MATHEMATICS, Dan Pedoe. Mathematical games, probability, the question of infinity, topology, how the laws of algebra work, problems of irrational numbers, and more. 42 figures. 143pp. 5⅜ × 8½. (EBE)
     22949-1 Pa. $3.50

READY-TO-USE DOLLHOUSE WALLPAPER, Katzenbach & Warren, Inc. Stripe, 2 floral stripes, 2 allover florals, polka dot; all in full color. 4 sheets (350 sq. in.) of each, enough for average room. 48pp. 8¼ × 11.   23495-9 Pa. $2.95

MINIATURE IRON-ON TRANSFER PATTERNS FOR DOLLHOUSES, DOLLS, AND SMALL PROJECTS, Rita Weiss and Frank Fontana. Over 100 miniature patterns: rugs, bedspreads, quilts, chair seats, etc. In standard dollhouse size. 48pp. 8¼ × 11.   23741-9 Pa. $1.95

THE DINOSAUR COLORING BOOK, Anthony Rao. 45 renderings of dinosaurs, fossil birds, turtles, other creatures of Mesozoic Era. Scientifically accurate. Captions. 48pp. 8¼ × 11.   24022-3 Pa. $2.25

JAPANESE DESIGN MOTIFS, Matsuya Co. Mon, or heraldic designs. Over 4000 typical, beautiful designs: birds, animals, flowers, swords, fans, geometrics; all beautifully stylized. 213pp. 11⅜ × 8¼. 22874-6 Pa. $7.95

THE TALE OF BENJAMIN BUNNY, Beatrix Potter. Peter Rabbit's cousin coaxes him back into Mr. McGregor's garden for a whole new set of adventures. All 27 full-color illustrations. 59pp. 4¼ × 5½. (Available in U.S. only) 21102-9 Pa. $1.50

THE TALE OF PETER RABBIT AND OTHER FAVORITE STORIES BOXED SET, Beatrix Potter. Seven of Beatrix Potter's best-loved tales including Peter Rabbit in a specially designed, durable boxed set. 4¼ × 5½. Total of 447pp. 158 color illustrations. (Available in U.S. only) 23903-9 Pa. $10.80

PRACTICAL MENTAL MAGIC, Theodore Annemann. Nearly 200 astonishing feats of mental magic revealed in step-by-step detail. Complete advice on staging, patter, etc. Illustrated. 320pp. 5⅜ × 8½. 24426-1 Pa. $5.95

CELEBRATED CASES OF JUDGE DEE (DEE GOONG AN), translated by Robert Van Gulik. Authentic 18th-century Chinese detective novel; Dee and associates solve three interlocked cases. Led to van Gulik's own stories with same characters. Extensive introduction. 9 illustrations. 237pp. 5⅜ × 8½. 23337-5 Pa. $4.50

CUT & FOLD EXTRATERRESTRIAL INVADERS THAT FLY, M. Grater. Stage your own lilliputian space battles.By following the step-by-step instructions and explanatory diagrams you can launch 22 full-color fliers into space. 36pp. 8¼ × 11. 24478-4 Pa. $2.95

CUT & ASSEMBLE VICTORIAN HOUSES, Edmund V. Gillon, Jr. Printed in full color on heavy cardboard stock, 4 authentic Victorian houses in H-O scale: Italian-style Villa, Octagon, Second Empire, Stick Style. 48pp. 9¼ × 12¼. 23849-0 Pa. $3.95

BEST SCIENCE FICTION STORIES OF H.G. WELLS, H.G. Wells. Full novel *The Invisible Man,* plus 17 short stories: "The Crystal Egg," "Aepyornis Island," "The Strange Orchid," etc. 303pp. 5⅜ × 8½. (Available in U.S. only) 21531-8 Pa. $4.95

TRADEMARK DESIGNS OF THE WORLD, Yusaku Kamekura. A lavish collection of nearly 700 trademarks, the work of Wright, Loewy, Klee, Binder, hundreds of others. 160pp. 8¾ × 8. (Available in U.S. only) 24191-2 Pa. $5.00

THE ARTIST'S AND CRAFTSMAN'S GUIDE TO REDUCING, ENLARGING AND TRANSFERRING DESIGNS, Rita Weiss. Discover, reduce, enlarge, transfer designs from any objects to any craft project. 12pp. plus 16 sheets special graph paper. 8¼ × 11. 24142-4 Pa. $3.25

TREASURY OF JAPANESE DESIGNS AND MOTIFS FOR ARTISTS AND CRAFTSMEN, edited by Carol Belanger Grafton. Indispensable collection of 360 traditional Japanese designs and motifs redrawn in clean, crisp black-and-white, copyright-free illustrations. 96pp. 8¼ × 11. 24435-0 Pa. $3.95

CHANCERY CURSIVE STROKE BY STROKE, Arthur Baker. Instructions and illustrations for each stroke of each letter (upper and lower case) and numerals. 54 full-page plates. 64pp. 8¼ × 11. 24278-1 Pa. $2.50

THE ENJOYMENT AND USE OF COLOR, Walter Sargent. Color relationships, values, intensities; complementary colors, illumination, similar topics. Color in nature and art. 7 color plates, 29 illustrations. 274pp. 5⅜ × 8½. 20944-X Pa. $4.50

SCULPTURE PRINCIPLES AND PRACTICE, Louis Slobodkin. Step-by-step approach to clay, plaster, metals, stone; classical and modern. 253 drawings, photos. 255pp. 8⅛ × 11. 22960-2 Pa. $7.50

VICTORIAN FASHION PAPER DOLLS FROM HARPER'S BAZAR, 1867-1898, Theodore Menten. Four female dolls with 28 elegant high fashion costumes, printed in full color. 32pp. 9¼ × 12¼. 23453-3 Pa. $3.50

FLOPSY, MOPSY AND COTTONTAIL: A Little Book of Paper Dolls in Full Color, Susan LaBelle. Three dolls and 21 costumes (7 for each doll) show Peter Rabbit's siblings dressed for holidays, gardening, hiking, etc. Charming borders, captions. 48pp. 4¼ × 5½. 24376-1 Pa. $2.25

NATIONAL LEAGUE BASEBALL CARD CLASSICS, Bert Randolph Sugar. 83 big-leaguers from 1909-69 on facsimile cards. Hubbell, Dean, Spahn, Brock plus advertising, info, no duplications. Perforated, detachable. 16pp. 8¼ × 11.
24308-7 Pa. $2.95

THE LOGICAL APPROACH TO CHESS, Dr. Max Euwe, et al. First-rate text of comprehensive strategy, tactics, theory for the amateur. No gambits to memorize, just a clear, logical approach. 224pp. 5⅜ × 8½. 24353-2 Pa. $4.50

MAGICK IN THEORY AND PRACTICE, Aleister Crowley. The summation of the thought and practice of the century's most famous necromancer, long hard to find. Crowley's best book. 436pp. 5⅜ × 8½. (Available in U.S. only)
23295-6 Pa. $6.50

THE HAUNTED HOTEL, Wilkie Collins. Collins' last great tale; doom and destiny in a Venetian palace. Praised by T.S. Eliot. 127pp. 5⅜ × 8½.
24333-8 Pa. $3.00

ART DECO DISPLAY ALPHABETS, Dan X. Solo. Wide variety of bold yet elegant lettering in handsome Art Deco styles. 100 complete fonts, with numerals, punctuation, more. 104pp. 8⅛ × 11. 24372-9 Pa. $4.00

CALLIGRAPHIC ALPHABETS, Arthur Baker. Nearly 150 complete alphabets by outstanding contemporary. Stimulating ideas; useful source for unique effects. 154 plates. 157pp. 8⅜ × 11¼. 21045-6 Pa. $4.95

ARTHUR BAKER'S HISTORIC CALLIGRAPHIC ALPHABETS, Arthur Baker. From monumental capitals of first-century Rome to humanistic cursive of 16th century, 33 alphabets in fresh interpretations. 88 plates. 96pp. 9 × 12.
24054-1 Pa. $4.50

LETTIE LANE PAPER DOLLS, Sheila Young. Genteel turn-of-the-century family very popular then and now. 24 paper dolls. 16 plates in full color. 32pp. 9¼ × 12¼. 24089-4 Pa. $3.50

KEYBOARD WORKS FOR SOLO INSTRUMENTS, G.F. Handel. 35 neglected works from Handel's vast oeuvre, originally jotted down as improvisations. Includes Eight Great Suites, others. New sequence. 174pp. 9⅜ × 12¼.
24338-9 Pa. $7.50

AMERICAN LEAGUE BASEBALL CARD CLASSICS, Bert Randolph Sugar. 82 stars from 1900s to 60s on facsimile cards. Ruth, Cobb, Mantle, Williams, plus advertising, info, no duplications. Perforated, detachable. 16pp. 8¼ × 11.
24286-2 Pa. $2.95

A TREASURY OF CHARTED DESIGNS FOR NEEDLEWORKERS, Georgia Gorham and Jeanne Warth. 141 charted designs: owl, cat with yarn, tulips, piano, spinning wheel, covered bridge, Victorian house and many others. 48pp. 8¼ × 11.
23558-0 Pa. $1.95

DANISH FLORAL CHARTED DESIGNS, Gerda Bengtsson. Exquisite collection of over 40 different florals: anemone, Iceland poppy, wild fruit, pansies, many others. 45 illustrations. 48pp. 8¼ × 11. 23957-8 Pa. $1.75

OLD PHILADELPHIA IN EARLY PHOTOGRAPHS 1839-1914, Robert F. Looney. 215 photographs: panoramas, street scenes, landmarks, President-elect Lincoln's visit, 1876 Centennial Exposition, much more. 230pp. 8⅜ × 11¾.
23345-6 Pa. $9.95

PRELUDE TO MATHEMATICS, W.W. Sawyer. Noted mathematician's lively, stimulating account of non-Euclidean geometry, matrices, determinants, group theory, other topics. Emphasis on novel, striking aspects. 224pp. 5⅜ × 8½.
24401-6 Pa. $4.50

ADVENTURES WITH A MICROSCOPE, Richard Headstrom. 59 adventures with clothing fibers, protozoa, ferns and lichens, roots and leaves, much more. 142 illustrations. 232pp. 5⅜ × 8½. 23471-1 Pa. $3.95

IDENTIFYING ANIMAL TRACKS: MAMMALS, BIRDS, AND OTHER ANIMALS OF THE EASTERN UNITED STATES, Richard Headstrom. For hunters, naturalists, scouts, nature-lovers. Diagrams of tracks, tips on identification. 128pp. 5⅜ × 8. 24442-3 Pa. $3.50

VICTORIAN FASHIONS AND COSTUMES FROM HARPER'S BAZAR, 1867-1898, edited by Stella Blum. Day costumes, evening wear, sports clothes, shoes, hats, other accessories in over 1,000 detailed engravings. 320pp. 9⅜ × 12¼.
22990-4 Pa. $9.95

EVERYDAY FASHIONS OF THE TWENTIES AS PICTURED IN SEARS AND OTHER CATALOGS, edited by Stella Blum. Actual dress of the Roaring Twenties, with text by Stella Blum. Over 750 illustrations, captions. 156pp. 9 × 12.
24134-3 Pa. $8.50

HALL OF FAME BASEBALL CARDS, edited by Bert Randolph Sugar. Cy Young, Ted Williams, Lou Gehrig, and many other Hall of Fame greats on 92 full-color, detachable reprints of early baseball cards. No duplication of cards with *Classic Baseball Cards.* 16pp. 8¼ × 11. 23624-2 Pa. $3.50

THE ART OF HAND LETTERING, Helm Wotzkow. Course in hand lettering, Roman, Gothic, Italic, Block, Script. Tools, proportions, optical aspects, individual variation. Very quality conscious. Hundreds of specimens. 320pp. 5⅜ × 8½.
21797-3 Pa. $4.95

HOW THE OTHER HALF LIVES, Jacob A. Riis. Journalistic record of filth, degradation, upward drive in New York immigrant slums, shops, around 1900. New edition includes 100 original Riis photos, monuments of early photography. 233pp. 10 × 7⅞. 22012-5 Pa. $7.95

CHINA AND ITS PEOPLE IN EARLY PHOTOGRAPHS, John Thomson. In 200 black-and-white photographs of exceptional quality photographic pioneer Thomson captures the mountains, dwellings, monuments and people of 19th-century China. 272pp. 9⅜ × 12¼. 24393-1 Pa. $12.95

GODEY COSTUME PLATES IN COLOR FOR DECOUPAGE AND FRAMING, edited by Eleanor Hasbrouk Rawlings. 24 full-color engravings depicting 19th-century Parisian haute couture. Printed on one side only. 56pp. 8¼ × 11. 23879-2 Pa. $3.95

ART NOUVEAU STAINED GLASS PATTERN BOOK, Ed Sibbett, Jr. 104 projects using well-known themes of Art Nouveau: swirling forms, florals, peacocks, and sensuous women. 60pp. 8¼ × 11. 23577-7 Pa. $3.50

QUICK AND EASY PATCHWORK ON THE SEWING MACHINE: Susan Aylsworth Murwin and Suzzy Payne. Instructions, diagrams show exactly how to machine sew 12 quilts. 48pp. of templates. 50 figures. 80pp. 8¼ × 11. 23770-2 Pa. $3.50

THE STANDARD BOOK OF QUILT MAKING AND COLLECTING, Marguerite Ickis. Full information, full-sized patterns for making 46 traditional quilts, also 150 other patterns. 483 illustrations. 273pp. 6⅞ × 9⅝. 20582-7 Pa. $5.95

LETTERING AND ALPHABETS, J. Albert Cavanagh. 85 complete alphabets lettered in various styles; instructions for spacing, roughs, brushwork. 121pp. 8¾ × 8. 20053-1 Pa. $3.75

LETTER FORMS: 110 COMPLETE ALPHABETS, Frederick Lambert. 110 sets of capital letters; 16 lower case alphabets; 70 sets of numbers and other symbols. 110pp. 8⅛ × 11. 22872-X Pa. $4.50

ORCHIDS AS HOUSE PLANTS, Rebecca Tyson Northen. Grow cattleyas and many other kinds of orchids—in a window, in a case, or under artificial light. 63 illustrations. 148pp. 5⅜ × 8½. 23261-1 Pa. $2.95

THE MUSHROOM HANDBOOK, Louis C.C. Krieger. Still the best popular handbook. Full descriptions of 259 species, extremely thorough text, poisons, folklore, etc. 32 color plates; 126 other illustrations. 560pp. 5⅜ × 8½. 21861-9 Pa. $8.50

THE DORÉ BIBLE ILLUSTRATIONS, Gustave Doré. All wonderful, detailed plates: Adam and Eve, Flood, Babylon, life of Jesus, etc. Brief King James text with each plate. 241 plates. 241pp. 9 × 12. 23004-X Pa. $8.95

THE BOOK OF KELLS: Selected Plates in Full Color, edited by Blanche Cirker. 32 full-page plates from greatest manuscript-icon of early Middle Ages. Fantastic, mysterious. Publisher's Note. Captions. 32pp. 9¾ × 12¼. 24345-1 Pa. $4.50

THE PERFECT WAGNERITE, George Bernard Shaw. Brilliant criticism of the Ring Cycle, with provocative interpretation of politics, economic theories behind the Ring. 136pp. 5⅜ × 8½. (Available in U.S. only) 21707-8 Pa. $3.00

CATALOG OF DOVER BOOKS

THE RIME OF THE ANCIENT MARINER, Gustave Doré, S.T. Coleridge. Doré's finest work, 34 plates capture moods, subtleties of poem. Full text. 77pp. 9¼ × 12. 22305-1 Pa. $4.95

SONGS OF INNOCENCE, William Blake. The first and most popular of Blake's famous "Illuminated Books," in a facsimile edition reproducing all 31 brightly colored plates. Additional printed text of each poem. 64pp. 5¼ × 7. 22764-2 Pa. $3.00

AN INTRODUCTION TO INFORMATION THEORY, J.R. Pierce. Second (1980) edition of most impressive non-technical account available. Encoding, entropy, noisy channel, related areas, etc. 320pp. 5⅜ × 8½. 24061-4 Pa. $4.95

THE DIVINE PROPORTION: A STUDY IN MATHEMATICAL BEAUTY, H.E. Huntley. "Divine proportion" or "golden ratio" in poetry, Pascal's triangle, philosophy, psychology, music, mathematical figures, etc. Excellent bridge between science and art. 58 figures. 185pp. 5⅜ × 8½. 22254-3 Pa. $3.95

THE DOVER NEW YORK WALKING GUIDE: From the Battery to Wall Street, Mary J. Shapiro. Superb inexpensive guide to historic buildings and locales in lower Manhattan: Trinity Church, Bowling Green, more. Complete Text; maps. 36 illustrations. 48pp. 3⅞ × 9¼. 24225-0 Pa. $2.50

NEW YORK THEN AND NOW, Edward B. Watson, Edmund V. Gillon, Jr. 83 important Manhattan sites: on facing pages early photographs (1875-1925) and 1976 photos by Gillon. 172 illustrations. 171pp. 9¼ × 10. 23361-8 Pa. $7.95

HISTORIC COSTUME IN PICTURES, Braun & Schneider. Over 1450 costumed figures from dawn of civilization to end of 19th century. English captions. 125 plates. 256pp. 8⅜ × 11¼. 23150-X Pa. $7.50

VICTORIAN AND EDWARDIAN FASHION: A Photographic Survey, Alison Gernsheim. First fashion history completely illustrated by contemporary photographs. Full text plus 235 photos, 1840-1914, in which many celebrities appear. 240pp. 6½ × 9¼. 24205-6 Pa. $6.00

CHARTED CHRISTMAS DESIGNS FOR COUNTED CROSS-STITCH AND OTHER NEEDLECRAFTS, Lindberg Press. Charted designs for 45 beautiful needlecraft projects with many yuletide and wintertime motifs. 48pp. 8¼ × 11. 24356-7 Pa. $1.95

101 FOLK DESIGNS FOR COUNTED CROSS-STITCH AND OTHER NEEDLE-CRAFTS, Carter Houck. 101 authentic charted folk designs in a wide array of lovely representations with many suggestions for effective use. 48pp. 8¼ × 11. 24369-9 Pa. $2.25

FIVE ACRES AND INDEPENDENCE, Maurice G. Kains. Great back-to-the-land classic explains basics of self-sufficient farming. The one book to get. 95 illustrations. 397pp. 5⅜ × 8½. 20974-1 Pa. $4.95

A MODERN HERBAL, Margaret Grieve. Much the fullest, most exact, most useful compilation of herbal material. Gigantic alphabetical encyclopedia, from aconite to zedoary, gives botanical information, medical properties, folklore, economic uses, and much else. Indispensable to serious reader. 161 illustrations. 888pp. 6½ × 9¼. (Available in U.S. only) 22798-7, 22799-5 Pa., Two-vol. set $16.45

DECORATIVE NAPKIN FOLDING FOR BEGINNERS, Lillian Oppenheimer and Natalie Epstein. 22 different napkin folds in the shape of a heart, clown's hat, love knot, etc. 63 drawings. 48pp. 8¼ × 11. 23797-4 Pa. $1.95

DECORATIVE LABELS FOR HOME CANNING, PRESERVING, AND OTHER HOUSEHOLD AND GIFT USES, Theodore Menten. 128 gummed, perforated labels, beautifully printed in 2 colors. 12 versions. Adhere to metal, glass, wood, ceramics. 24pp. 8¼ × 11. 23219-0 Pa. $2.95

EARLY AMERICAN STENCILS ON WALLS AND FURNITURE, Janet Waring. Thorough coverage of 19th-century folk art: techniques, artifacts, surviving specimens. 166 illustrations, 7 in color. 147pp. of text. 7⅞ × 10¾. 21906-2 Pa. $9.95

AMERICAN ANTIQUE WEATHERVANES, A.B. & W.T. Westervelt. Extensively illustrated 1883 catalog exhibiting over 550 copper weathervanes and finials. Excellent primary source by one of the principal manufacturers. 104pp. 6⅛ × 9¼. 24396-6 Pa. $3.95

ART STUDENTS' ANATOMY, Edmond J. Farris. Long favorite in art schools. Basic elements, common positions, actions. Full text, 158 illustrations. 159pp. 5⅜ × 8½. 20744-7 Pa. $3.95

BRIDGMAN'S LIFE DRAWING, George B. Bridgman. More than 500 drawings and text teach you to abstract the body into its major masses. Also specific areas of anatomy. 192pp. 6½ × 9¼. (EA) 22710-3 Pa. $4.50

COMPLETE PRELUDES AND ETUDES FOR SOLO PIANO, Frederic Chopin. All 26 Preludes, all 27 Etudes by greatest composer of piano music. Authoritative Paderewski edition. 224pp. 9 × 12. (Available in U.S. only) 24052-5 Pa. $7.50

PIANO MUSIC 1888-1905, Claude Debussy. Deux Arabesques, Suite Bergamesque, Masques, 1st series of Images, etc. 9 others, in corrected editions. 175pp. 9⅜ × 12¼. (ECE) 22771-5 Pa. $5.95

TEDDY BEAR IRON-ON TRANSFER PATTERNS, Ted Menten. 80 iron-on transfer patterns of male and female Teddys in a wide variety of activities, poses, sizes. 48pp. 8¼ × 11. 24596-9 Pa. $2.25

A PICTURE HISTORY OF THE BROOKLYN BRIDGE, M.J. Shapiro. Profusely illustrated account of greatest engineering achievement of 19th century. 167 rare photos & engravings recall construction, human drama. Extensive, detailed text. 122pp. 8¼ × 11. 24403-2 Pa. $7.95

NEW YORK IN THE THIRTIES, Berenice Abbott. Noted photographer's fascinating study shows new buildings that have become famous and old sights that have disappeared forever. 97 photographs. 97pp. 11⅜ × 10. 22967-X Pa. $6.50

MATHEMATICAL TABLES AND FORMULAS, Robert D. Carmichael and Edwin R. Smith. Logarithms, sines, tangents, trig functions, powers, roots, reciprocals, exponential and hyperbolic functions, formulas and theorems. 269pp. 5⅜ × 8½. 60111-0 Pa. $3.75

HANDBOOK OF MATHEMATICAL FUNCTIONS WITH FORMULAS, GRAPHS, AND MATHEMATICAL TABLES, edited by Milton Abramowitz and Irene A. Stegun. Vast compendium: 29 sets of tables, some to as high as 20 places. 1,046pp. 8 × 10½. 61272-4 Pa. $19.95

CATALOG OF DOVER BOOKS

REASON IN ART, George Santayana. Renowned philosopher's provocative, seminal treatment of basis of art in instinct and experience. Volume Four of *The Life of Reason*. 230pp. 5⅜ × 8.
24358-3 Pa. $4.50

LANGUAGE, TRUTH AND LOGIC, Alfred J. Ayer. Famous, clear introduction to Vienna, Cambridge schools of Logical Positivism. Role of philosophy, elimination of metaphysics, nature of analysis, etc. 160pp. 5⅜ × 8½. (USCO)
20010-8 Pa. $2.75

BASIC ELECTRONICS, U.S. Bureau of Naval Personnel. Electron tubes, circuits, antennas, AM, FM, and CW transmission and receiving, etc. 560 illustrations. 567pp. 6½ × 9¼.
21076-6 Pa. $8.95

THE ART DECO STYLE, edited by Theodore Menten. Furniture, jewelry, metalwork, ceramics, fabrics, lighting fixtures, interior decors, exteriors, graphics from pure French sources. Over 400 photographs. 183pp. 8⅜ × 11¼.
22824-X Pa. $6.95

THE FOUR BOOKS OF ARCHITECTURE, Andrea Palladio. 16th-century classic covers classical architectural remains, Renaissance revivals, classical orders, etc. 1738 Ware English edition. 216 plates. 110pp. of text. 9½ × 12¾.
21308-0 Pa. $11.50

THE WIT AND HUMOR OF OSCAR WILDE, edited by Alvin Redman. More than 1000 ripostes, paradoxes, wisecracks: Work is the curse of the drinking classes, I can resist everything except temptations, etc. 258pp. 5⅜ × 8½. (USCO)
20602-5 Pa. $3.50

THE DEVIL'S DICTIONARY, Ambrose Bierce. Barbed, bitter, brilliant witticisms in the form of a dictionary. Best, most ferocious satire America has produced. 145pp. 5⅜ × 8½.
20487-1 Pa. $2.50

ERTÉ'S FASHION DESIGNS, Erté. 210 black-and-white inventions from *Harper's Bazar*, 1918-32, plus 8pp. full-color covers. Captions. 88pp. 9 × 12.
24203-X Pa. $6.50

ERTÉ GRAPHICS, Erté. Collection of striking color graphics: *Seasons, Alphabet, Numerals, Aces* and *Precious Stones*. 50 plates, including 4 on covers. 48pp. 9⅜ × 12¼.
23580-7 Pa. $6.95

PAPER FOLDING FOR BEGINNERS, William D. Murray and Francis J. Rigney. Clearest book for making origami sail boats, roosters, frogs that move legs, etc. 40 projects. More than 275 illustrations. 94pp. 5⅜ × 8½.
20713-7 Pa. $2.25

ORIGAMI FOR THE ENTHUSIAST, John Montroll. Fish, ostrich, peacock, squirrel, rhinoceros, Pegasus, 19 other intricate subjects. Instructions. Diagrams. 128pp. 9 × 12.
23799-0 Pa. $4.95

CROCHETING NOVELTY POT HOLDERS, edited by Linda Macho. 64 useful, whimsical pot holders feature kitchen themes, animals, flowers, other novelties. Surprisingly easy to crochet. Complete instructions. 48pp. 8¼ × 11.
24296-X Pa. $1.95

CROCHETING DOILIES, edited by Rita Weiss. Irish Crochet, Jewel, Star Wheel, Vanity Fair and more. Also luncheon and console sets, runners and centerpieces. 51 illustrations. 48pp. 8¼ × 11.
23424-X Pa. $2.00

YUCATAN BEFORE AND AFTER THE CONQUEST, Diego de Landa. Only significant account of Yucatan written in the early post-Conquest era. Translated by William Gates. Over 120 illustrations. 162pp. 5⅜ × 8½.   23622-6 Pa. $3.50

ORNATE PICTORIAL CALLIGRAPHY, E.A. Lupfer. Complete instructions, over 150 examples help you create magnificent "flourishes" from which beautiful animals and objects gracefully emerge. 8⅛ × 11.   21957-7 Pa. $2.95

DOLLY DINGLE PAPER DOLLS, Grace Drayton. Cute chubby children by same artist who did Campbell Kids. Rare plates from 1910s. 30 paper dolls and over 100 outfits reproduced in full color. 32pp. 9¼ × 12¼.   23711-7 Pa. $3.50

CURIOUS GEORGE PAPER DOLLS IN FULL COLOR, H. A. Rey, Kathy Allert. Naughty little monkey-hero of children's books in two doll figures, plus 48 full-color costumes: pirate, Indian chief, fireman, more. 32pp. 9¼ × 12¼.
24386-9 Pa. $3.50

GERMAN: HOW TO SPEAK AND WRITE IT, Joseph Rosenberg. Like *French, How to Speak and Write It.* Very rich modern course, with a wealth of pictorial material. 330 illustrations. 384pp. 5⅜ × 8½. (USUKO)   20271-2 Pa. $4.75

CATS AND KITTENS: 24 Ready-to-Mail Color Photo Postcards, D. Holby. Handsome collection; feline in a variety of adorable poses. Identifications. 12pp. on postcard stock. 8¼ × 11.   24469-5 Pa. $2.95

MARILYN MONROE PAPER DOLLS, Tom Tierney. 31 full-color designs on heavy stock, from *The Asphalt Jungle,Gentlemen Prefer Blondes,* 22 others.1 doll. 16 plates. 32pp. 9⅜ × 12¼.   23769-9 Pa. $3.50

FUNDAMENTALS OF LAYOUT, F.H. Wills. All phases of layout design discussed and illustrated in 121 illustrations. Indispensable as student's text or handbook for professional. 124pp. 8⅛.× 11.   21279-3 Pa. $4.50

FANTASTIC SUPER STICKERS, Ed Sibbett, Jr. 75 colorful pressure-sensitive stickers. Peel off and place for a touch of pizzazz: clowns, penguins, teddy bears, etc. Full color. 16pp. 8¼ × 11.   24471-7 Pa. $2.95

LABELS FOR ALL OCCASIONS, Ed Sibbett, Jr. 6 labels each of 16 different designs—baroque, art nouveau, art deco, Pennsylvania Dutch, etc.—in full color. 24pp. 8¼ × 11.   23688-9 Pa. $2.95

HOW TO CALCULATE QUICKLY: RAPID METHODS IN BASIC MATHE-MATICS, Henry Sticker. Addition, subtraction, multiplication, division, checks, etc. More than 8000 problems, solutions. 185pp. 5 × 7¼.   20295-X Pa. $2.95

THE CAT COLORING BOOK, Karen Baldauski. Handsome, realistic renderings of 40 splendid felines, from American shorthair to exotic types. 44 plates. Captions. 48pp. 8¼ × 11.   24011-8 Pa. $2.25

THE TALE OF PETER RABBIT, Beatrix Potter. The inimitable Peter's terrifying adventure in Mr. McGregor's garden, with all 27 wonderful, full-color Potter illustrations. 55pp. 4¼ × 5½. (Available in U.S. only)   22827-4 Pa. $1.60

BASIC ELECTRICITY, U.S. Bureau of Naval Personnel. Batteries, circuits, conductors, AC and DC, inductance and capacitance, generators, motors, trans-formers, amplifiers, etc. 349 illustrations. 448pp. 6½ × 9¼.   20973-3 Pa. $7.95

CATALOG OF DOVER BOOKS

SOURCE BOOK OF MEDICAL HISTORY, edited by Logan Clendening, M.D. Original accounts ranging from Ancient Egypt and Greece to discovery of X-rays: Galen, Pasteur, Lavoisier, Harvey, Parkinson, others. 685pp. 5⅜ × 8½.
20621-1 Pa. $10.95

THE ROSE AND THE KEY, J.S. Lefanu. Superb mystery novel from Irish master. Dark doings among an ancient and aristocratic English family. Well-drawn characters; capital suspense. Introduction by N. Donaldson. 448pp. 5⅜ × 8½.
24377-X Pa. $6.95

SOUTH WIND, Norman Douglas. Witty, elegant novel of ideas set on languorous Meditterranean island of Nepenthe. Elegant prose, glittering epigrams, mordant satire. 1917 masterpiece. 416pp. 5⅜ × 8½. (Available in U.S. only)
24361-3 Pa. $5.95

RUSSELL'S CIVIL WAR PHOTOGRAPHS, Capt. A.J. Russell. 116 rare Civil War Photos: Bull Run, Virginia campaigns, bridges, railroads, Richmond, Lincoln's funeral car. Many never seen before. Captions. 128pp. 9⅜ × 12¼.
24283-8 Pa. $6.95

PHOTOGRAPHS BY MAN RAY: 105 Works, 1920-1934. Nudes, still lifes, landscapes, women's faces, celebrity portraits (Dali, Matisse, Picasso, others), rayographs. Reprinted from rare gravure edition. 128pp. 9⅜ × 12¼. (Available in U.S. only)
23842-3 Pa. $6.95

STAR NAMES: THEIR LORE AND MEANING, Richard H. Allen. Star names, the zodiac, constellations: folklore and literature associated with heavens. The basic book of its field, fascinating reading. 563pp. 5⅜ × 8½.
21079-0 Pa. $7.95

BURNHAM'S CELESTIAL HANDBOOK, Robert Burnham, Jr. Thorough guide to the stars beyond our solar system. Exhaustive treatment. Alphabetical by constellation: Andromeda to Cetus in Vol. 1; Chamaeleon to Orion in Vol. 2; and Pavo to Vulpecula in Vol. 3. Hundreds of illustrations. Index in Vol. 3. 2000pp. 6⅛ × 9¼.
23567-X, 23568-8, 23673-0 Pa. Three-vol. set $36.85

THE ART NOUVEAU STYLE BOOK OF ALPHONSE MUCHA, Alphonse Mucha. All 72 plates from *Documents Decoratifs* in original color. Stunning, essential work of Art Nouveau. 80pp. 9⅜ × 12¼.
24044-4 Pa. $7.95

DESIGNS BY ERTE; FASHION DRAWINGS AND ILLUSTRATIONS FROM "HARPER'S BAZAR," Erte. 310 fabulous line drawings and 14 *Harper's Bazar* covers, 8 in full color. Erte's exotic temptresses with tassels, fur muffs, long trains, coifs, more. 129pp. 9⅜ × 12¼.
23397-9 Pa. $6.95

HISTORY OF STRENGTH OF MATERIALS, Stephen P. Timoshenko. Excellent historical survey of the strength of materials with many references to the theories of elasticity and structure. 245 figures. 452pp. 5⅜ × 8½. 61187-6 Pa. $8.95